MAHATMA GANDHI
THE CONGRESS
AND
THE PARTITION OF INDIA

MAHATMA GANDHI
THE CONGRESS AND THE PARTITION OF INDIA

D. C. Jha

KW Publishers Pvt Ltd
New Delhi

KNOWLEDGE WORLD

KW Publishers Pvt Ltd
4676/21, First Floor, Ansari Road, Daryaganj, New Delhi 110002
✉ knowledgeworld@vsnl.net ✆ +91.11.23263498/43528107

www.kwpub.com

All rights reserved. No part of this book may be reproduced or transmitted in any form or by any means, electronic or mechanical, including photocopying, recording or by any information storage and retrieval system, without permission in writing.

First Published 1995	ISBN 81-703-031-2
Second Edition 2004	ISBN 81-87943-466
Third Edition 2009	ISBN 81-87416-83-1
Fourth Edition 2014	ISBN 978-93-83649-03-7

© 2014, DC Jha

In Praise of
Mahatma Gandhi The Congress and The Partition of India

You have strung together authentic accounts and made an irrefutable presentation. I wish many people read it. I am sure it will help in removing many misunderstandings, at least in those who are willing to see.

RavindraVarma
Chairman
Gandhi Peace Foundation
New Delhi

D. C. Jha lets incontestable documents tell the story. He should be commended for uniting several threads into a pattern of irony, tragedy and heroism that does justice to history. A valuable book.

Prof. Rajmohan Gandhi
Gandhi Marg
New Delhi

The book is a treat. The assiduous assembly of facts and informed comments on the events leading to partition are admirable. This journey through a crucial period of our history should be of immense help to the present generation as also for future generations.

L. C. Jain
Member of Planning Commission
Government of India

There are many aspects of partition, covered in the book, about which I was not fully aware. I found the book immensely readable and illuminating.

Prof. N. C. Nigam
Vice Chancellor
Roorkee University (U.P.)

The book is a scholarly presentation of the events of that time. It will prove to be an asset for both the general reader and the serious students of freedom struggle.

The Tribune
Chandigarh (Punjab)

I have read D.C. Jha's intimate memoire of Mahatma Gandhi and the Congress and the prelude to India's partition with unflagging interest and recommend his book to all serious students of Indian history. Mr. Jha is to be congratulated for his honesty and fearless integrity.

Prof. S.A. Wolpert
Professor of Indian History
University of California
Los Angles, USA

It is a very interesting study of the struggle over Partition. D.C. Jha has done a service to offer vigorous defense of Gandhi's vision and of the departure of the Congress leaders from the vision upon their accession to political power. It is a powerful and tragic tale.

Prof. James Hunt
Gandhian Scholar,
North Carolina, USA

The book makes a vital and a valuable contribution to understanding the urgent importance of Gandhi's message for India today.

Prof. Dennis Dalion
Barnard Collage
Columbia University
New York

Dedicated to My Parents

S.K. Jha and Savitri Devi

Both of whom passed away five and thirty-five years before this book was first published in the year 1995.

Contents

	Foreword by Dr. Sushila Nayar	xi
	Introduction by the Author	xvii
1.	Second World War and Indian Independence	3
2.	Quit India: The Unlaunched Battle	15
3.	Prelude to Partition	33
4.	Gandhi and Partition	53
5.	Congress Breaches Gandhi's Trust	61
6.	Gandhi Considered Partition Preventable	67
7.	British Infamy Led to Partition	75
8.	Gandhi and the Congress	86
	(i) Afterword	103
	(ii) Facsimile of Gandhi's letter to President Roosevelt	107
	(iii) Photo of Gandhi at Sodepur Ashram	
	Appendix I Gandhi's Last Will & Testament	109
	Appendix II Exchange of letters between Gandhi & Satis Mukerji and Dr. Rajendra Prasad and Satis Mukerji	112
	Appendix III British Prime Minister's Statement Regarding Transfer of Power by June 1948	118
	Appendix IV Preface to Second Edition by Dr. Mohan Dharia	121
	References	125

Let not the coming generations curse Gandhi for being a party to India's vivisection.

— Mahatma Gandhi

Foreword to the First Edition

It is a fact universally recognised that India owes her freedom to Gandhiji. Had it not been for the helmsmanship he provided to the country for an unbroken period of thirty years, it is a moot point whether India would have steered her course to national independence in the comparatively short time than she did.

Indeed it was Gandhiji, more than any other individual or group of individuals, who first breathed the spirit of freedom into the oppressed masses of India and awakened them to the realisation that their salvation lay in throwing off the British yoke and taking in their own hands the threads of their national destiny. It was he, above all others, who gave voice to the inchoate aspirations of the dumb millions of our country and inspired in them the dream of a society in which citizens would be fearless and free, of a polity in which villages would be self-improving, selfsufficient and self-governing units of a commonwealth organised on the principles of love and non-violence and having no use for arms or armies.

To bring into being that freedom, that kingdom of God, Gandhiji needed an instrument. He fashioned the Congress into one. The Congress, it is true, had existed before Gandhiji's appearance on the scene but it had existed, notwithstanding brief and localised spurts of militancy, represented by such as Tilak, primarily as an organisation of lawyers and other elite, who saw the place of India within the British empire and found their own *raison d'etre* in every now and then submitting petitions to the rulers for paltry political and economic concessions.

Gandhiji took the organisation in his hands and gave it the baptism of fire. He made it the mouthpiece of the masses and the vanguard in the struggle for freedom. Titanic movements followed—all non-violent—the Congress in the forefront: the anti-Rowlatt Act campaign, the Khilafat movement, the Non-cooperation movement, the Simon boycott campaign, salt satyagraha movement of 1930 and civil disobedience revival in 1932, the individual civil disobedience movement, and finally, the Quit India movement. The last named, it is true, was not organised by Gandhiji or the Congress, but the spirit of defiance that the masses manifested during the movement, their dogged and determined refusal to recognise British authority as legitimate or lawful, was certainly inspired by Gandhiji. From each of these movements the Congress emerged a stronger, purer and more authentic representative of the masses, a ready instrument to wrest independence from unwilling hands.

But though Gandhiji was primarily responsible for bringing freedom to the country, he was not responsible for the partition, which was the price paid for the freedom. He opposed the dismemberment of the country on communal lines to the very last. He opposed, too, the partitioning of the Punjab and Bengal. He was not responsible for the evil consequences of the partition: the insensate, fratricidal carnage that started on August 16, 1946 with Jinnah's "direct action" and continued uninterrupted until Gandhiji's martyrdom, taking a toll of half a million lives and opening the sluice gates for the mass exodus of population in untold numbers. Other forces and individuals than Gandhiji were responsible for the tragic turmoil and carnage that accompanied freedom, preceded by partition of India.

While others ignited the fire and fuelled the flames, Gandhiji strove with all his might to douse them wherever he could. Soon after the formation of the Interim Government—the first ever government deserving to be called national, though still functioning under the Viceroy—Gandhiji was in Noakhali, trudging from village to village, trying to bring hope and comfort to the victims of the "direct action," preaching the message of communal peace, love and non-violence, putting courage in the hearts of the minorities and making the majority aware of their duty towards them.

Again when independence was proclaimed in August 1947, he was not in Delhi to join in the celebrations, He was away in Calcutta, mourning for the dead of both the communities, organising relief for the displaced and the dispossessed, praying and fasting for sanity to be restored and peace to be brought back to Calcutta and the village and towns of Bengal and Bihar.

The pre- and post-partition carnage and the complex economic, social and human problems it threw up in both India and Pakistan, were thus the doing of forces and drives, ambition and power hunger of men, which, notwithstanding his superhuman efforts Gandhiji had not been able to tame even in the Congress, and which found their full play when state power appeared to be within grasp.

Shri D. C. Jha has unfolded the tragic story and brought out clearly and convincingly, citing chapter and verse, how Gandhiji strove with all his might to prevent the tragedy which led to the uprooting of millions of men, women and children from both sides of the boundary. A perusal of the work will help the reader to grasp the complex issues engaging the minds of political leaders involved in the deliberations and parley that resulted in the transfer of power and creation of India and Pakistan. He will also at once see where the guilt lies for the historical crime of partition, as a result of which hundreds of thousands lost their lives and the widows and orphans on both sides made a mockery of independence.

The story of Gandhiji's efforts to save the unity of India is as fascinating as his conduct of the freedom struggle. He never wanted anything for himself. He lived for India and he wanted to see a united India free of foreign rule. All his striving were directed towards upliftment of the downtrodden, removal of poverty, hunger, filth and insanitation. He wanted to see each village evolve into a prosperous, happy unit, with maximum political and economic independence and yet a part of the total organism—India; as each cell of the human body is an integral part of it. He tried his best to explain his point of view to the Indian leaders, but impatient for power they were more inclined to listen to the bureaucracy and the Viceroy, Lord Mountbatten, than to the man who had led them to freedom. They were afraid he might want them to take another dose of self-denial, to make more sacrifices and even to go back to jail. They were "tired old men" and they did not wish to lose the opportunity to rule India. They probably genuinely believed that they would be able to rebuild India into a prosperous, happy nation.

Nehru, the virtual Prime Minister, though called Vice President of the Interim Government, had grown up under Western influence and he could only think of adopting the Western model. He had often expressed his differences with Gandhiji over the years during the freedom struggle, but in the past he had always given in to Gandhiji's judgment in the end and accepted his decision. That was not the case after he joined the government. After assuming power, he was far less inclined to consult Gandhiji or listen to him. This process had already started before he had become Vice President of the Interim Government.

Gandhiji was away on his mission of mercy putting out the flames of communal hatred in Noakhali and elsewhere. He was a broken man. His desire to live for 125 years had gone. He would often say, "I cannot bear it any more. '0' God, take me away." But his success in restoring human values with his healing touch wherever he went, gave him new hope.

Gandhiji had come to Delhi on the summons of Mountbatten. He had spent three months in Noakhali and two months in Bihar before coming to Delhi.

The British had consistently played the game of divideand-rule and always advanced the plea of Hindu-Muslim differences for not loosening their hold on India. During the war Churchill had rejected with contempt the advice of the President of the USA, his own colleagues and Chiang Kai-shek as well as others, such as the Prime Ministers of Canada and Australia.

The Congress-League coalition Government was not functioning as a team. When Mountbatten consulted Gandhiji, he told him to give power to one party. Gandhiji was prepared to give power to Jinnah and seemed confident that the Congress leaders would agree. After all, Hindus and Muslims were children of mother India. He pleaded with the Vicerory that the British Government should not divide India but leave it to the Indians to do it, if necessary, after the British were gone. He urged the Viceroy to hand over the government to Muslim League supremo M. A. Jinnah.

Mountbatten was tempted by the idea. It would have been one more feather in his cap. Nothing however came out of it. The advisers of the Viceroy considered the proposal unworkable. The Congress leaders gave it short shrift. Mountbatten had been able to persuade Nehru and Patel to accept the idea of partition while Gandhiji was away from Delhi after first round of talks with the Viceroy.

I remember vividly how shocked Gandhiji had been when Nehru, J. B. Kripalani and Mridula Sarabhai came to report to Gandhiji why they had agreed to the division of the Punjab on communal lines, which became prelude to partition of India. They had talked with Gandhiji alone. As they came out, I could see Gandhiji's haggard face. He said to Kripalani, "Professor, even you did not think that Bapu should be consulted?" It was like the fallen

Julius Caesar looking up and saying, "Et tu, Brute!" What could Kripalani or anyone else say.

India, though free at last, was cut up, bleeding and crying out in agony. Heartbroken, Gandhiji was in Calcutta on August 15 trying to extinguish the communal flames of hatred by fasting. He was successful. Mountbatten called him the one-man boundary force who could manage the situation single-handed on the eastern front, which an armed force of 55,000 was not able to do on the western.

Gandhiji returned to Delhi intent on undertaking another monumental enterprise. He wanted to take the Hindus and Sikhs to Lahore as they had fled from west Punjab in hundreds of thousands, and bring back the Muslims from there, who had gone from Delhi and elsewhere in India. "The land is divided," he said, "but let the hearts not be divided." He summoned Pyarelal, whom he had left behind in Noakhali. But God had other plans. On January 30 he fell to Godse's bullet. His death shook the world. The leaders in India and Pakistan were staggered into repentance and settlement of certain disputes between the Prime Ministers of India and Pakistan followed. His martyrdom made both the sides reasonable for a while.

Ever since the partition, India and Pakistan have had daggers drawn. Their mutual relations have been marked by continuous suspicion, distrust and even hatred. They have fought three wars against each other. Meanwhile people in both countries remain victims of unrelieved poverty, violence, lack of education, lack of sanitation and widespread discontent. Fundamentalism is raising its ugly head.

If only the last Viceroy had heeded Bapu's advice or if only the "tired old men" of the Congress had the patience to wait a little while longer and follow their leader as they had done in the past, India might have been spared the agony. It would have been able to show to the world the miracle of developing a nation, with happy, prosperous, clean, educated, pious and honest men and women, living peacefully in its 700,000 villages. No heavy expenditure on arms and armaments, imports of foreign goods, and domination by western influence and heavy debts would have accumulated. On the contrary India might have presented a model to the West of "earth in balance" as Al Gore, the Vice President of the USA, has pictured in his book which bears that title—*Earth in Balance*—sustainable development.

But God is great. There can still be hope. Therefore, let us hope and pray that India and Pakistan will turn a new leaf and undo the mischief. Britain may well have divided India because it did not want India to be strong and equal to it. We can still find a way together to do better than them by following the path shown by Gandhiji. But the question is when shall we have the wisdom to do so.

New Delhi
February 21, 1995

Sushila Nayar

Introduction

The first edition of this book came out in 1995. The second edition followed eight years later at the end of 2003. That edition had the privilege of being released to the public by Dr. Manmohan Singh, then the Leader of the Opposition in the Upper House of Indian Parliament, but soon to take over as the Prime Minister of India in 2004. The present volume is the fourth edition of the book, with additional documents, information and comments spread over almost all the chapters of the book.

It has been a matter of great satisfaction to me that the book had received praise from a large cross section of serious readers in India and abroad. It is my hope that they may find the fourth edition of the book meeting their expectations too.

The Hindi edition of the book came out soon after the first English edition was published. It was released by the then Vice President of India, Shri Krishna Kant. The Marathi and Bengali editions followed in quick succession to each other. Finally the Gujarati edition came out, thus making the book available in four Indian languages as well.

* * *

I grew up in one of the Ashrams near Calcutta, which also served as Mahatma Gandhi's headquarters during his visits to Bengal and Assam. Besides coming in contact with the Mahatma during his stays in this Ashram at Sodepur, I was fortunate to be included, as a young man of twenty, in the group that accompanied Mahatma Gandhi to Noakhali (now in Bangladesh) after the communal riots that shook that district in October 1946, following the Great Calcutta Killings that took place a couple of months earlier in August.

It was a rare privilege, too, for me to be entrusted with the responsibility of taking Mahatma Gandhi's letter to, and bringing back to Noakhali reply from Dr. Rajendra Prasad about post-riot situation and scenario of Bihar, which continued to worry the Mahatma in Noakhali.

It was a bitterly cold winter morning of December when I arrived at Dr. Rajendra Prasad's residence in Patna. I was called in as soon as he was told that a messenger had arrived with a letter from the Mahatma. I had come straight from the railway station and it was still very dark.

As he went through the letter, Dr. Rajendra Prasad showed signs of worry. He spoke to the Chief Minister and the Finance Minister asking them to come over for a meeting after briefing them about the Mahatma's letter. And he asked me to join the meeting as well. Soon after an early morning meeting with the ministers, he wrote his reply and handed me the letter to take it to the Mahatma.

This was not the first time that I had met Dr. Rajendra Prasad. I had been his house-guest in New Delhi only a couple of months earlier. He had by then become a member of the Interim Government and I had carried to him a letter from Satish Chandra Das Gupta, the head of the Ashram at Sodepur, seeking help from his Department for the relief work he was overseeing in the nearby villages.

My stay with Dr. Rajendra Prasad in Delhi led to yet another development. His autobiography had come out during those days and copies of the book were available at his residence. While glancing through the book on my return journey to Calcutta, I noted that Dr. Rajendra Prasad had written an essay in 1930 on "non-violence" which he had passed on to his former teacher Satis Chandra Mukerji to glance through. Satis Mukerji had been the doyen of Swadeshi movement, who had taken charge of Mahatma Gandhi's weekly journal *Young India* when Gandhiji and others had been imprisoned. Dr. Prasad had mentioned in his autobiography that he did not remember what happened to that essay as soon afterwards he along with others had been taken to the prison during non-cooperation movement, and he had forgotten all about it by the time he came out of prison.

I mentioned this fact to my father on my return to the Ashram. My father had been a life-long devotee of Satis Chandra Mukerji, with whom he had maintained a regular and steady correspondence over the years. He drew his mentor's attention to what I had brought to his notice. It resulted in digging out of the manuscript from heaps of old files. Father received instruction that he should get a fair typed copy made of the essay and then send it to Dr. Prasad.

The exchange of letters that followed—between the master Satis Mukerji and his old student Dr. Rajendra Prasad—have been included in the book for topical interest. Correspondence that took place during those days between the Mahatma and Satis Mukerji has also been included in the book for its great significance.

These contacts with Dr. Rajendra Prasad, then a member of the Interim Government but soon to take over as the President of the Constituent Assembly and later to become the first President of India, led fortunately for me in development of a lasting and affectionate relationship with him. And my contact with Mahatma Gandhi's Secretary Pyarelal during Mahatma's stays in Sodepur Ashram resulted later, in 1950, in my joining and assisting Pyarelal in writing and publication of the two volumes of *Mahatma Gandhi—The Last Phase*, in the series of his planned multivolume biography of the Mahatma.

* * *

As a young man I had thus been eye-witness to the partition of the country, and to the interplay of forces and events that led to the great tragedy; how Mahatma Gandhi fought to prevent partition to the very last and why and how the Congress leaders allowed the British to divide the country against the Mahatma's advice and pleading. This book was therefore conceived to put under a concise cover broad overview of that traumatic event for the generations that followed, who at best may have only a vague and hazy notion of what and how this tragic event took place.

I have begun the narrative of the book in the background of the Second World War (1939-44), as it was a distinct watershed in the Indo-British relationship.

For my source, I had taken the help of the twelve volumes of the *Transfer of Power*, published by the British Government, *The Life of Mahatma Gandhi* by Louis Fischer, *Mahatma Gandhi—The Last Phase* by Pyarelal, *The Discovery of India* by Jawaharlal Nehru and *Freedom at Midnight* by Dominic Lapierre and Larry Collins.

I acknowledge my indebtedness to the authors and publishers of these books, as also to the authors and publishers of some other books and articles, acknowledgment for which have been made under "References."

I wish to put on record once again my gratitude for the encouragement I received for writing the book from I. P. Anand, a friend and a senior colleague in Thapar House; for the guidance I got for publication of first edition from B. R. Bowry of the Indian Information Service; for valuable suggestions I received for the publication of the third edition of the book from L. C. Jain, a friend and a former Deputy Chairman of the Planning Commission, and to Gandhi Memorial Trust for the financial support extended to facilitate publication of the first edition of the book in 1995.

New Delhi
December 2013

D. C. Jha

Do not be angry with me if I tell the truth

—Socrates

1

Second World War and Indian Independence

"I have not become His Majesty's First Minister in order to preside over the liquidation of the British Empire." This was how Winston Churchill had announced his policy for India after he had taken over as the Prime Minister of Great Britain in the wake of humiliating defeat and withdrawal of the British Army from continental Europe in the early phase of the Second World War.

India was the brightest "jewel in the crown" of the British Empire. Churchill had always considered its freedom from British rule as an unmitigated disaster for the English people. He had "through the years made numerous statements against Indian independence," Louis Fischer, the well-known American journalist and author, had recorded. "He now had the power to prevent it as the Prime Minister of Great Britain."

Churchill's "perception" of India was based on "his experience in Bangalore in the reign of Queen Victoria as a subaltern in the British cavalry regiment," stated Philip Mason, who was Secretary to Chiefs of Staff Committee in Delhi during the Second World War. "Churchill was a great man," he said, "not a just man ... And he did not understand India."

It was in Bangalore that Churchill had "discovered the Empire first-hand; the glittering privileges of the British Raj, then at the height of its power and glory," his biographer Norman Rose had noted. And even when times and conditions had changed beyond recognition, in the 1930s and 1940s, Churchill was "still bent on preserving the image of the Empire he was forewed as a young subaltern" that Britain had "inherited the world as of right by virtue of her superior power."

"He has a curious complex about India and always loaths to hear good of it and apt to believe the worst," noted General Wavell, the Commander-in-Chief of India, in his journal about Churchill.

Churchill used all his authority as the Prime Minister, and every argument and means at his disposal, to frustrate attempts from any quarter to make him deviate from, or persuade him to change, his India policy even at the time of the biggest crisis for and greatest threat to the British Empire—be it from his Deputy Prime Minister Clement Attlee or from the head of the wartime Chinese ally Marshal Chiang Kai-shek, or even from President Roosevelt of the United States of America, his strongest supporter in the war against Germany and Japan. In pursuing his "India policy," Churchill had his staunchest supporters in the Viceroy Lord Linlithgow in Delhi and the Secretary of State for India, Leopold Amery in London.

Within two years of breaking out of the war in Europe in 1939, Japan brought it to Asia with a surprise and stunning strike on American Pacific Fleet based in Honolulu in Hawai Islands, destroying a large number of warships and killing several thousand civilians and military personnel. In a very short period thereafter, and without encountering much resistance, it then took over large parts of South-east Asia, defeating French in Indo-China (now Vietnam), Dutch in Dutch East-Indies (now Indonesia) and the Americans in the Philippines.

After quickly sinking two British warships—Prince of Wales and Repulse—at Singapore harbour, the Japanese forced the British garrison there to surrender without resistance. Pushing the British army up the Malay Peninsula, the Japanese army soon arrived at the Burma border. Rangoon fell not much later. By early 1942, the British had thus left its "loyal subjects" in all those countries to fend for themselves. Even in this bleak situation one finds the Viceroy of India serving the following fare to British Prime Minister and his cabinet colleagues in London.

"We are frequently urged to do something 'to touch the heart' of India," said Linlithgow in his message of January 21. "But the Cabinet will I think agree with me that India and Burma have no natural association with the Empire, from which they are alien by race, history and religion, and for which as such neither of them have any natural affection, and both are in the Empire because they are conquered countries which have been brought there by force, kept there by our controls, and which hitherto it had suited to remain under our protection."

The threat of invasion of India by then, however, loomed large and the British Press and public opinion had begun to clamour that "the danger in the Far East made a settlement of the Indian question necessary." A debate on India in the British Parliament had thus become unavoidable. Even in that grave situation Linlithgow was advising London that with regard to the "suggestion that we should ... accept the demand for full independence and give tangible proof of the reality of our doing so, it seems to me to be out of the question to consider anything of the sort ... I would rather face such trouble as we may have to face here as a result of making no concessions now in the political field than make concessions ..."[1]

Noting, however, that "His Majesty's Government will naturally wish to appear as constructive as possible in any debate," the Viceroy went on to give the classic advice that the "general line of any debate could properly be that we have responsibilities to discharge and pledges to honour; to harp again on the depth and reality of Indian differences; to insist that in no circumstances shall we go back on our pledges to the Muslims; to bring out the incompatibility of the Muslim League demands with those of the Congress ... On these lines I should hope that we could regain any ground which Congress has taken from us by the appearance of readiness to cooperate (in war efforts) on reasonable terms ..."[2]

When a copy of the Viceroy's communication reached him, Deputy Prime Minister Clement Attlee felt outraged. In a note he told his Cabinet colleagues that he found it quite impossible "to accept and act on the crude imperialism of the Viceroy, not only because I think it is wrong, but because I think it is fatally short-sighted and suicidal. I should certainly not be prepared to cover up this ugliness with a cloak of pious sentiment about liberty and democracy ... I do consider that now is the time for an act of statesmanship."[3]

Disagreeing with the conclusion arrived at by the Viceroy and the Secretary of State for India that "nothing can or should be done at the present time," Attlee added: "This seems to me to result from a dangerous ignoring of the present situation ... India has been profoundly affected by the changed relationship between Europeans and Asiatics ... The reverses which we and Americans are sustaining from the Japanese at the present time will continue this process."[4]

"The fact that we are now accepting Chinese aid in our war ... and necessarily driven to a belated recognition of China as an equal and of Chinese as fellow-fighters for civilisation against barbarism," Attlee went on to remind his colleagues, "makes the Indian ask why he, too, cannot be the master in his own house ... We are condemned by Indians not by the measure of Indian ethical conceptions but our own, which we have taught them to accept. It is precisely this acceptance by politically conscious Indians of the principles of democracy and liberty which puts us in a position of being able to appeal to them to take part with us in the common struggle; but the success of this appeal and India's response does put upon us the obligation of seeing that we ... make them share in the things for which we and they are fighting."[5]

While this drama was unfolding, Churchill received a message from his Ambassador Clark Kerr in Chungking, the wartime Chinese capital, that Marshal Chiang Kai-shek intended to pay a visit to India "to get in personal touch with the Viceroy and to see Gandhi and Nehru ... and to impress on them essential wisdom of cooperating fully for the common cause."[6]

In another message the Ambassador informed London that the Chinese were "grumbling too about ... disturbing echoes...contrasting President of United States' deliverance and independence of Philippines with the absence of any kindred declaration by ourselves that might give Indians something to hope for and fight for ... Chinese criticism about (India) is harsh and persistent. They accuse us of insincerity."[7] This was nothing less than a ton of bricks being dropped on Churchill.

"With regard to your seeing persons like Mr. Gandhi and Mr. Nehru, who are in a state at least of passive disobedience to the King Emperor, this you will readily see is a matter which requires very grave consideration ..." read Churchill's reply to Chiang through Ambassador Clark Kerr. "In any case, if you begin seeing the leaders of the Indian Congress Party, it would be necessary that you should also see Mr. Jinnah representing 80,000,000 Moslems, and representatives of the 40,000,000 depressed classes and of the Indian Princes who rule over 80,000,000 ..."[8] It was necessary for Churchill to educate Chiang that Gandhi, Nehru and the Congress did not represent even half the Indian population, and that half did not include Muslims or depressed classes or those who lived in the Princely states!

The British Ambassador in Chungking felt concerned that delivering Churchill's message would make an extremely bad impression on Chiang. "There is much in the form and text which in the present circumstances it would be unnecessary and even injudicious to convey" to Chiang Kai-shek, Clark Kerr wrote back. Chiang's purpose in visiting India, he told London, was "to see the recalcitrants (read Gandhi and Nehru) in the firm belief that his personal influence upon them would serve the common cause. Any suggestion made at this stage which would cast a doubt upon his good faith and discretion ... would I fear make a most painful impression. I am, therefore, concerned to hear ... that instructions have been received in Delhi to dissuade Chiang Kai-shek from his purpose. This would I think be a very grave mistake."⁹

While leaving it to Clark Kerr whether his message in amended form should be delivered to Chiang or not, Churchill at the same time directed the Viceroy in Delhi that "if you could bring about the desired result without showing him (Chiang) the actual text of the message, there is no objection to your withholding it ... (However) do not hesitate to use the message if there is any real necessity for it."¹⁰

The Viceroy of course had no difficulty in dealing with the situation the way Churchill wanted it to be handled. "I made it very clear to Clark Kerr," reported Linlithgow to London, "that I had no intention of allowing the Chinese to go to Wardha (to meet Gandhi) or to Allahabad (to see Nehru). I explained ... that for good political reasons we could not tolerate a visit of this kind and ... that if the Marshal could not be dissuaded from his visit, I intended, even at the risk of offending him, to prevent him from going ... I have taken steps to prevent the Generalissimo from obtaining transport to Wardha whether by train, air or road, and ... it is my firm intention to compel him to respect my wishes in this regard."¹¹

If he did not fall in line, the Head of China and a wartime ally was not to be treated in any better way. The utmost Linlithgow was prepared to go to make it possible for Chiang to speak to Indian leaders was "to communicate ... with Messrs Jinnah and Gandhi to suggest their coming to Delhi in order to meet the Marshal."¹² The Viceroy had earlier informed London that "I shall have to coax him to receive the head of the Muslim League whether he feels inclined to or not."¹³ It was made abundantly clear that Chiang had to see Jinnah if he wanted to meet Gandhi.

Chiang had thus to meet Jinnah as required by the British, and Gandhi had to travel to Calcutta from Wardha to see the Marshal when he was on his way back to China. Chiang, however, could see through the game the British were playing with him and with the Indians. "I sincerely hope and confidently believe," he said in his farewell statement, "that our ally Great Britain, without waiting for any demands on the part of people of India, will as speedily as possible give them real political power, so that they may ... realise that their participation in war is not merely an aid to anti-aggression nations for securing victory, but also a turning point in their struggle for India's freedom."¹⁴

Churchill had no intention to heed any such advice. Chiang, however, continued to press his point with the British as well as with the Americans since he considered "the political situation in India grave, not because of the fear that Congress will help Japanese but because without the vital impulse for active freedom, which alone is worth fighting for, Japanese invasion of India will not encounter rigid resistance ... (and) in the absence of effective realistic stimulus Indian morale will show little resilience."[15]

Reporting his talk with the Chinese Foreign Minister Dr. T. V. Soong, whose sister was Chiang's wife, the Canadian Prime Minister Mackenzie King informed Churchill that in a communication which Soong had received, Chiang had stated that "he doubted if Britain could count on the necessary support in India to save the situation there unless immediate actions were taken to ensure to India full dominion status" and that Chiang Kai-shek felt that "the alleged difficulties which arise between Mohammedans and Hindus had been greatly exaggerated." Chiang was convinced that it would be difficult "to save the existing situation which he regarded as extremely precarious" unless self-government problem could be met immediately. "You no doubt have this information which Soong had communicated to United States Government and possibly also to the British Ambassador."[16]

"We believe," wrote Mackenzie King in another telegram to Churchill, "that a fully self-governing India has a great part to play in free and equal association with the other nations of the British Commonwealth and that a free India fighting alongside the other free people will strengthen immeasurably the common cause."[17]

In answer to his suggestion regarding self-governing India and report about his talk with Chinese Foreign Minister Soong, the Canadian Prime Minister received the following from Churchill: "Question which has to be solved is not between British Government and India, but between different sects or nations in India itself ... Congress have hitherto definitely refused dominion status. Moslems, a hundred millions, declare they will insist upon Pakistan ... We have our treaties which must be respected with Princes in India, over ninety million. There are forty million Hindu untouchables to whom we have obligations ... There can be no question of our handing over control during the war."[18]

To put the growing American anxiety about India at rest, however, Churchill informed President Roosevelt that "we are earnestly considering whether a declaration of dominion status after the war ... should be made at this critical juncture." He took care at the same time to repeat to Roosevelt what he had told the Canadian Prime Minister, namely that "we must not on any account break with the Moslems ... We have also to consider our duty towards ... untouchables and our treaties with the Princes' states of India ... Naturally we do not want to throw India into chaos on the eve of invasion."[19]

* * *

These arguments and the excuses did not cut much ice with President Roosevelt as they had not done earlier with Marshal Chiang Kai-shek. "I have given much thought to India ... I have felt much diffidence in making any suggestion ... I have tried to approach the problem from the point of view of history ..." wrote back President Roosevelt. "That is why I go back to the inception of the Government of the United States with a hope that injection of a new thought to be used in India might be of assistance to you."[20]

He reminded Churchill that during the American Revolution between 1775 and 1783 the British colonies had set themselves up as thirteen states, each one under a different form of government. But at the end of the war, in 1783, with the British "it was clear that the new responsibilities of the thirteen sovereignties could not be welded into a federal union ... Therefore, the thirteen sovereignties joined in the Articles of Confederation, an obvious stopgap government, to remain in effect only until such times as experience and trial and error could bring about a permanent union." This arrangement proved, however, through lack of federal power that they would soon fly apart into separate nations. Therefore, "in 1787 a Constitutional Convention was held ... representing all the states. They met, not as a parliament, but as a small group of sincere patriots, with the sole objective of establishing a federal government ... The present constitution of the United States resulted and soon received the assent of two-thirds of the states."

"It is merely a thought of mine to suggest the setting up of what might be called a temporary Government of India," advised President Roosevelt, "headed by a small representative group, covering different castes, occupations, religions and geographies—this group to be recognised as a temporary Dominion Government. It would, of course, represent existing Governments of the British provinces and would also represent the Council of Princes, but my principal thought is that it would be charged with setting up a body to consider a more permanent Government for the whole country ... Perhaps the analogy of some such method to the travails and problems of the United States from 1783 to 1789 might give a new slant in India itself, and it might cause the people there to forget hard feelings ... together with the advantage of peaceful evolution as against chaotic revolution. Such a move is strictly in line with the world changes of the past half century and with the democratic process of all who are fighting Nazism."

These arguments too had no effect on Churchill. Writing in *The Times* of London, John Chemley had noted that "Churchill tended to forget who had won the American war of independence." The American had carried down the years an abiding dislike of imperialism because of their experience as a British colony. But Churchill "ignored the political reality of an America which did not share his belief in Britain's glorious destiny as an imperialist ... world power."

However as a result of all these goings-on, in which issues had been joined not only by his own Deputy Prime Minister Attlee and the Commonwealth Prime Minister of Canada but also by Chiang Kai-shek and President Roosevelt, and after many permutations and combinations of a number of schemes and formulations, Churchill decided to send to India Sir Stafford Cripps, a member of the Cabinet, to try to enlist the active cooperation of all elements of the Indian national life in the war effort on the basis of a scheme worked out undoubtedly with great ingenuity but without conceding to India anything substantial, much less anything resembling self-government or the Government to be formed under the scheme to be treated at par with other dominion governments within the British Commonwealth.

Cripps was "of course bound by the draft Declaration which is our utmost limit," Churchill said in his telegram to the Viceroy. "If that is rejected by the Indian parties ... our sincerity will be proved to the world ... It would be impossible, owing to ... the general American outlook, to stand on a purely negative attitude and the Cripps Mission is (therefore) indispensable to prove our honesty of purpose and gain time ... ."[21]

The drama had to be enacted to gain time and to satisfy world opinion, in particular that of America. The Cripps Mission was doomed to fail because Cripps had been provided with a scheme to which he was not authorised to make any substantial modifications to meet even the minimum Indian aspirations. The scheme did not offer any political or decision-making power to Indians even on the basis of acceptable convention. Cripps had been directed to persuade acceptance of the scheme; not to negotiate with Indians to make it acceptable. "You speak of carrying on negotiations," read Churchill's telegram to Cripps in Delhi. "It was certainly agreed between us all that there were not to be negotiations but that you were to try to gain acceptance with possible minor variations."[22]

Knowing what the scheme contained, the Secretary of State for India was advising the Canadian Prime Minister, even before Cripps had arrived in India, to stay his hand in appointing a High Commissioner to Delhi "until we know the Cripps Mission has succeeded or failed. Personally, I fear that the latter is the more probable alternative, and that the Congress will reject our policy because it does not give Indian political leaders the immediate control of the conduct of the war."[23]

In their very first meeting, Gandhi had told Cripps that "it would have been better if he had not come to India with a cut and dried scheme to impose upon India," and questioned the retention of defence in British hands.[24] Gandhi advised Cripps to return home by the "first available plane" if the scheme he had shown him was all that he had come to offer.

With the views that Churchill held, it was insane for anyone to expect that the British would offer anything of substance to India or allow Cripps to negotiate to come to a satisfactory or acceptable settlement. It must be recorded in fairness that Cripps did try for an acceptable settlement but found his hands tied by Churchill. The problem had been compounded further by the Viceroy's inability to support Cripps and by his briefing London to convey his differences. "Your telegram ... apparently refers to some sent from here which I have not seen," read one of Cripps' telegrams to London, "and therefore I find difficulty in understanding them ... I am sorry my colleagues appear to distrust me ... Unless I am trusted I cannot carry on with the task."[25]

In three successive letters Maulana Abul Kalam Azad, the Congress President, had made the Congress position clear and had also recorded the clarifications and assurances given by Cripps. "We are interested as you know," he wrote in one of these letters, "in ... full popular control of defence ... We consider such control essential before responsibility can be undertaken ... Problems of higher strategy may well be controlled by Inter-Allied Cabinet or Council, but the effectual control of the defence of India should rest with the Indian National Government." In another letter Azad put on record that "in our talks you gave us to understand that you envisaged a National Government which would deal with all matters except defence." And finally: "In the course of our talks—you had referred ... to a National Government and a Cabinet consisting of ministers—and we had imagined that the new government would function with full powers as a Cabinet with the Viceroy acting as a constitutional head ..."[26]

Cripps later found to his dismay that he was in no position to stand by his assurances. He failed to get the support of the Viceroy and the British

Government was not willing to treat the Government to be formed under the scheme as a National Government nor to agree that there "should be definite assurances and conventions which would indicate that the new government would function as a free government."

"I was left with a strong impression," the Viceroy reported to the Secretary of State in London, "that Cripps in his extreme anxiety to meet Congress claims and secure the support from them which might have resulted in securing the support of other parties, may have taken chances in discussions which were dangerous, and I am confirmed in that view by statements such as those positively made by ... Azad ... that Cripps had talked very freely of a National Government presided over by the Viceroy who would stand in much the same relation to it as the King does at home."[27]

"Scraps of information that come to me ... are leading me a little to wonder," Linlithgow wrote to Amery in his next communication, "whether the Congress had not after all some reason to think that His Majesty's Government and the Cabinet were prepared to go practically the whole way as regards the Viceroy's Council, leaving the Viceroy in the position of constitutional monarch, and whether they may not quite genuinely have thought that Cripps was prepared to make such a concession and to go to those lengths, and with that assumption in view, concentrated on the one outstanding point of defence."[28]

On learning that Cripps had failed in his mission, President Roosevelt felt deeply concerned. He directed his personal representative in London, Harry Hopkins, to urgently convey a message from him to Churchill because "every effort must be made by us to prevent a break-down."

"I regret to say," Roosevelt made it clear in his telegram to Churchrill, "that I am unable to agree with the point of view contained in your message to me, that public opinion in the United States believes that negotiations have broken down on general broad issues. Here the general impression is quite to the contrary. The feeling is held almost universally that the deadlock has been due to the British Government's unwillingness to concede the right of self-government to the Indians notwithstanding the willingness of the Indians to entrust to the competent British authorities technical military and naval defence control. It is impossible for American public opinion to understand why, if there is willingness on the part of the British Government to permit the component parts of India to secede after the war from the British Empire, it is unwilling to permit them to enjoy during the war what is tantamount to self-government."

"I feel that I am compelled to place before you this issue very frankly," President Roosevelt added, "and I know you will understand my reasons for doing this. Should the current negotiations be allowed to collapse because of the issue as presented to the people of America ... it would be hard to overestimate the prejudicial reaction on American public opinion."

Roosevelt, therefore, advised Churchill to have Cripps' departure from India postponed on the ground that "you have personally transmitted instructions to him to make a final effort to find a common ground of understanding. According to my reading, an agreement appeared very near last Thursday night. If you could authorise him to say that he was personally empowered by you to resume negotiations as at that point... it appears to me that an agreement might yet be found."[29]

Churchill of course had no intention to follow Roosevelt's advice to empower Cripps to negotiate with Indian leaders for a common ground of understanding. "About 3 a.m. this morning ... the text of your message to me about India came through from London," read Churchill's reply to Roosevelt from Chequers. "I could not decide such a matter without convening the Cabinet, which was not physically possible till Monday ... I did not feel I could take responsibility for the defence of India if everything has again to be thrown into the melting pot at this critical juncture. That I am sure would be the view of Cabinet and of Parliament."[30]

Taking shelter behind the facade that the telegram was not addressed to him as the Prime Minister, Churchill informed Roosevelt that he was treating his message "as purely private" and therefore "I do not propose to bring it before the Cabinet." The message he had received from Washington and the reply that Churchill sent were thus kept a closely guarded secret. "As regards Roosevelt, Prime Minister tells me he has communicated with him, and no further action is required," the Secretary of State for India recorded.[31] And "determined efforts supported by Number Ten (Downing Street) have failed to extract from the Prime Minister what he has said to the President."[32]

Having been itself a colony of Britain in the past, "the United States understood India's aspiration despite the propaganda fog" created by the British, Louis Fischer had recorded. And Harry Hopkins had said, wrote Robert E. Sherwood in his book *Roosevelt and Hopkins*, that "he did not think that any suggestions from the President to the Prime Minister in the entire war were so wrathfully received as those relating to the solution of the Indian problem."[33]

"One of Churchill's closest and most affectionate associates had said to me," Harry Hopkins had himself recorded, "the President might have known that India was the one subject on which Winston would never move a yard."[34]

Attempts from every conceivable quarter to meet the Indian aspirations were thus frustrated and the Indian question was successfully put under the lid by Churchill. It was only several years later that Clement Attlee, as the post-war Prime Minister of Great Britain, was able to initiate fresh attempts to tackle the India question. He subsequently also located a person in Lord Mountbatten, "to do in India what Durham did in Canada" to save Canada for the British Empire.

Mountbatten not only succeeded in forcing partition on India at a breakneck speed against all logic and sane consideration, with the consent of the Indian leaders, but also prevailed upon them that they could get full power in their hands a few months earlier than the planned transfer of power if they consented to keep the country as a dominion within the British Commonwealth.

* * *

This is, however, anticipating events. What the British did immediately after Cripps' departure from Delhi was to ban the publication of the resolutions adopted by the Congress, one of which criticised the administration for the panic and incompetence demonstrated by inefficient and irresponsible officials in dealing with the grave situation that the country faced due to anticipated Japanese invasion, and for the "recent extraordinary happenings in Burma and notably in the city of Rangoon, when though actual military operations were still some distance away, the entire civil administration suddenly collapsed and those in charge of it sought their own safety and abandoned their posts just when their presence was most needed."[35]

2

Quit India: The Unlaunched Battle

"As the war approaches India," the Congress stated in its resolution, publication of which the government had banned, "the lessons of Rangoon and Lower Burma are full of meaning for this country, for the same type of officials wield authority here, and recent astonishing exhibition of panic and incompetence in Madras demonstrates dangers arising from inefficient and irresponsible officials, who have, in addition, no contact with the people of the country."

"It is the misfortune of India at this crisis in her history," the resolution went on to record, "not only to have foreign government but a government which is incompetent and incapable of organising her defence properly or of providing for the safety and essential needs of her people."

The reference to exhibition of panic and incompetence related to the sudden moving of government offices and High Court from the city of Madras to various places in the interior after an air-raid alarm and expected Japanese landing in the coastal south India. This led to heavy and rapid exodus of population from the city. A similar exodus had taken place from the towns of Visakhapatnam and Kakinada which had experienced similar air raids and had suffered a large number of casualties and where people faced great difficulty in securing essential items of food, etc.

Drawing attention to these dismal facts, the resolution further stated that "recent orders passed and circulars issued on behalf of various Provincial governments indicate that they are obsessed with making provision for safety of higher civil officials and their removal from the place of immediate danger. Little thought appears to have been given to drawing up of well-prepared schemes for possible evacuation of a particular area and arrangement of transport, housing and food supply in a time of emergency."

Defending the banning of the Congress resolution, the Government of India explained to London that "we realise that our action may provoke conflict with large section of Press and possibly with Congress itself" but "we are convinced that time has come to stem the flood of seditious and defeatist utterances with which the Congress are endeavouring to cover the failure over Cripps Mission."[1]

The boot was, however, on the other foot. The Congress had no reason to "endeavour" to cover the failure of the Cripps Mission. It had realised quite early that the intention of the British Cabinet in sending the proposals with Cripps was not sincere but was merely intended as a facade before the world; and although Cripps had felt disappointed at not being able to stand by his commitments made in his negotiations with the Congress leaders, his explanation about the reasons of breakdown was intended to serve as political propaganda among the United Nations.

Churchill had told Harry Hopkins that Cripps had "presented a new proposal to Nehru without consultation with the Governor-General (Viceroy)." It was perfectly clear, Hopkins later recorded, "that the Governor-General was irritated with the whole business." The Viceroy "telegraphed Churchill. Churchill ordered Cripps to withdraw the new ... proposals and return to England."[2]

This was further confirmed by Colonel Louis Johnson, President Roosevelt's personal representative in India, who had helped Cripps in working out the new formula. On finding that "discussions were likely to result in settlement" on the basis of new proposals put forward by Cripps, Churchill "telegraphed that His Majesty's Government would not ratify" unless the Commander-in-Chief (Wavell) and the Viceroy telegraphed directly to him that they agreed, and as Wavell and Linlithgow refused to do so, "negotiations broke down."[3]

Cripps was in India during the first fortnight of April and the Congress resolution was banned at the end of April 1942.

* * *

Two and a half years earlier at the beginning of the war in September 1939, Mahatma Gandhi had announced that he would not take any steps to embarrass the British Government; he would even extend his moral support to England and her allies in their hour of distress. He disapproved of war; even so he had to make a distinction between aggressor and defender. He blamed Hitler for the war. His sympathy was, therefore, with the English and French.

The Congress went even one step further. It expressed its willingness to actively support the war efforts if certain conditions were met. If self-rule was granted to India, said the Congress, "a free, democratic India will gladly associate herself with the free nations for mutual defence against aggression ..."[4]

Gandhi was opposed to such bargaining. "Whatever support was to be given to the British," he said, "should be given unconditionally" and of course non-violently. Even so, he commended the Congress resolution and explained the apparent inconsistency in the following words: "I would not serve the cause of non-violence if I deserted my best co-workers because they could not follow me in an extended application of non-violence. I, therefore, remain with them in the faith that their departure from the non-violent method will be confined to the narrowest field and will be temporary."

The British were, however, in no mood to grant selfgovernment even to get active support of the Congress in Britain's war effort. The maximum they could get, said Linlithgow, was a greater share for Indians in the Viceroy's Executive Council.

Gandhi had no use for such an offer; neither had the Congress. But despite Gandhi's disapproval, Congress went ahead to adopt a resolution, sponsored by Rajagopalachari, to express once again its eagerness that if India were given independence "it will enable the Congress to throw its full weight in the efforts for the effective organisation of the defence of the country."

If Gandhi had so desired, Rajagopalachari would have withdrawn his resolution. But Gandhi would not take that step. "That would have been dictation ... Gandhi believed too much in personal liberty to exploit his power to make men vote or act against their will." Gandhi would prefer "to break with the Congress rather than break its leader."[5] But Gandhi felt unhappy, "unhappy because my word seemed to lose the power to carry with me those whom it was my proud privilege to carry all these many years."[6]

The Viceroy's response to this repeat offer by the Congress was to reiterate that he would invite more Indians to join his Executive Council. More ominous was his statement that the British Government could not transfer their responsibilities to any Indian government whose authority was directly denied by large segments of the population. It was for the first time that the British openly gave the minority community a veto on India's political future.

The Congress felt thoroughly incensed. It accused the British Government of rejecting its friendly and patriotic offer of cooperation and making the issue of the minorities an insuperable barrier to India's progress. The Congress leaders realised too the futility of repeatedly offering cooperation in war efforts in exchange of self-rule and then finding their offer turned down with contempt. They returned to the Mahatma once again.

"Whenever Congress rejected Gandhi's pacifism and volunteered to aid the British," noted Louis Fischer, Gandhi "did not interfere. Whenever Congress agreed with him and wanted to hinder the war effort, he objected."[7]

"I do not want England to be defeated or humiliated," Gandhi said in a speech soon after. "It is not because I love the British nation and hate the Germans. I do not think that Germans as a nation are any worse than the English ... We are all tarred with the same brush ... I cannot claim any superiority for Indians ... I can keep India intact and its freedom intact only if I have goodwill towards the whole of the human family and not merely for the human family which inhabits this little spot of the earth called India."

He would tell the Viceroy, said Gandhi, that "we do not want to embarrass you" or to "deflect you from your purpose in regard to the war effort." But the people and the Congress could not forgo their right of freedom of speech and expression of views. "If we carry the people with us, there will be no war effort on the part of our people. If, on the other hand, without using any but moral pressure, you find that people help the war effort, we can have no cause for grumbling. If you get assistance ... from anybody, high or low, you can have it, but let our voice also be heard."

To get the voice of India heard by the world without launching a mass civil disobedience movement, which would have hindered the British war efforts, Gandhi decided on a symbolic way to defy the official ban on propaganda against the war. He would select individuals to do so one after the other, one at a time. The person so chosen would defy the ban after intimating the administration of the date, the place and the time of doing so in advance.

Vinoba Bhave, one of his closest associates, was selected by Gandhi to be the first to offer individual satyagraha, followed by Nehru, Sardar Patel and Pyarelal, Gandhi's own secretary. Nehru was sentenced to four years' imprisonment for defying the ban and Patel was arrested even before he could make his speech. To allow the British officers to enjoy Christmas, as a goodwill gesture Gandhi suspended the movement for ten days. A total of over 23,000 people from all over the country defied the ban over the next one year, were arrested and put into prison.

The political scene changed dramatically once Japan entered the war in December 1941, crippling the British naval presence in the Indian Ocean by sinking two battle ships in Singapore harbour, and rapidly and menacingly advancing towards the Indian border after throwing out with lightning speed British forces from Malaya, Singapore and Burma. It was in this backdrop that the British Cabinet had sent Cripps to India in April 1942. The Cripps Mission had awakened hopes that the British might allow the Indians to become masters of their destiny. But that was not to be.

"It is time the door is finally closed after the repeated insults heaped upon us," remarked Sardar Patel in the Congress Working Committee meeting on the failure of the Cripps Mission and the kind of statements that were issued by the British Government blaming the Congress, even though the Congress had gone to the farthest in its endeavour to accommodate the British viewpoint for the duration of the war.[8]

During the months of May, June and July of 1942 "thousands of Indian refugees were straggling out of Burma to escape the conquering Japanese," wrote Louis Fischer. "England apparently lacked the strength to protect India from invasion. Vocal Indians were irritated and exasperated by their utter helplessness ... Tension was mounting; but Indians had no voice and no power to act."[9]

The All-India Congress Committee met to take stock of the situation. "In view of the imminent peril of invasion that confronts India," it stated, "and the attitude of the British Government as shown again in the recent proposals sponsored by Sir Stafford Cripps, the AICC has to declare afresh India's policy ... The policy of the British Government ... has demonstrated that even in this hour of danger, not only to India but to the cause of the United Nations, the British Government functions as an imperialist Government and refuses to recognise the independence of India, or to part with any real power ... If India were free, she would have determined her own policy ... to join the war ... as a free country fighting for freedom, and her defence would have been organised on a popular basis with a national army under national control ... Not only the interest of India but also Britain's safety and world peace and freedom demand that Britain must abandon her hold on India."[10]

By banning publication of the Congress resolution, the British had chosen a collision course; to provoke conflict with the Congress and to administer a rebuff to the Indian people. Gandhi would neither accept the rebuff nor feel helpless. "Gandhi found the situation intolerable. He believed and had taught a vast following that Indians must shape their own destiny."[11]

"I remain the same friend of the British today that I was at the beginning of the war," wrote Gandhi in his weekly journal *Harijan*, of May 10, 1942.

"I am convinced that the time has come during the war, not after it, for the British and Indians to be reconciled to complete separation from each other. Estrangement between them is growing."

Gandhi followed it by adding that he was "watching and trying ... to educate public opinion about my demand for withdrawal of the British from India. I am trying to show that behind this demand there is no ill-will. It is a logical and friendly act in the interest of all. I am moving cautiously, not thoughtlessly, but with fixed determination."[12]

Next, in a lead article in *Harijan* of May 17, Gandhi asked every Briton "to support me in my appeal to the British ... to retire ... from India. That step is essential for the safety of the world and for destruction of Nazism, Fascism and Japan's 'ism' which is a good copy of the other two ... British statesmen talk glibly of India's participation in the war. India was never even formally consulted on declaration of war. Why should it? India does not belong to Indians but to the British ... Britain may be said to be at perpetual war with India, which she holds by right of conquest and through an army of occupation."

Gandhi followed this by explaining a week later, in *Harijan* of May 24, that there was "confusion in some minds about my invitation to the British to withdraw. India has no quarrel with British people. I have hundreds of British friends. Andrews' friendship was enough to tie me to the British people. But we were both fixed in determination that British rule in India in any shape or form must end ... I invite every Britisher who loves Britain, India and the world to join me in an appeal to British power."

"Early in the week I spent at the ashram in June 1942," Louis Fischer had noted, "it became obvious that Gandhi was determined to launch a civil disobedience campaign with a view to make England 'Quit India.'"[13] But Gandhi had no objection to the British army operating from India for the duration of the war once they had withdrawn their rule from India. "Britain and America, and other countries too, can keep their armies here and use Indian territory as a base for military operation. I do not wish Japan to win the war ... I do not wish to humiliate England ... They could operate the railways ... They would need order in the ports where they received their supplies ... These matters would require cooperation and common effort."[14]

The response of the Secretary of State for India to Gandhi's various statements, which the Viceroy had regularly been cabling to the British Government, was to advise Linlithgow that if Gandhi and the Congress leaders were "really prepared ... to embark on a policy of real mischief, then I hope you do not hesitate or lose a moment in acting firmly and swiftly. Don't refer to me if you want to arrest Gandhi or any of them, but do it and I shall back you up."[15]

"It is quite likely," wrote Linlithgow to Amery, "that if the old man (Gandhi) finds that he cannot get behind him the degree of support that he would like, he will think better of his proposed campaign. But his influence is so great and he carries so much weight in the country that he may well by himself be able to turn the scale that would otherwise be doubtful ..."[16]

And again: "The old man has lost none of his political skill with age ... I think he is still, as I have always thought him, the one man capable of uniting all the various threads of thought in the Congress, and I find it difficult to conceive of circumstances in which any lengthy resistance to him on the part of Congress leaders, however prominent, can be looked for."[17]

"Make no mistake about it," the Viceroy had told Louis Fischer. "The old man is the biggest thing in India ... His influence is very great."[18]

Gandhi was convinced that "India should be granted self-government during the war; if the anti-Axis powers did not understand this, he would call it to their attention by a civil disobedience campaign."[19] But there were quite a few dissenting voices within the Congress to launching of a mass civil disobedience movement. Nehru's first reaction was unfavourable. So was that of the Congress President Azad. With logic Gandhi, however, convinced them that the movement was essential if the country was not to lose its soul.

Gandhi's mind was not closed to arguments against launching of the movement. "If anybody could convince me," he told A. T. Steele of the *New York Herald Tribune*, "that in the midst of war the British Government cannot declare India free without jeopardising the war effort, I should like to hear the argument." And in answer to Steele's question, "If you were convinced, would you call off the campaign?" the Mahatma had replied: "Of course. My complaint is that all these good people talk .1t me, swear at me, but never condescend to talk to me."[20]

Louis Fischer had recorded that "1942 was Churchill's first opportunity in office to cope with a civil disobedience movement in India. The British Government preferred suppression to discussion."[21] The Viceroy had talked to Gandhi in 1939 and in 1940 but not thereafter since Churchill had taken over as the Prime Minister.

In the midst of all these hectic activities and engagements, Gandhi could however find time to inquire about the welfare of the Viceroy's family. "When you write to them," Gandhi wrote to Linlithgow in his letter of July 2, 1942, "please send my regards to Lady Anne and Southby. I hope they and the baby are getting on well."[22]

Replied the Viceroy by return of post: "Very many thanks indeed for your kind personal message for my daughter Lady Anne and Southby. They will much appreciate it and I am passing it on to them at once. We have a photo of Richard, now about a year old, that shows him to be a fine fellow."[23]

But the Viceroy had also by then taken the decision to arrest and put under detention Gandhi and all top Congress leaders as soon as the Congress resolved to launch the civil disobedience movement.

* * *

In the first week of July Gandhi wrote to President Roosevelt of USA, and to General Chiang Kai-shek, the Chinese supremo, to put at rest any misgivings that the leaders of the Allied nations might have about the proposals he had put forward for immediate withdrawal of the British rule from India.

Addressing the President as "dear friend," Gandhi introduced himself to Roosevelt in the following words: "I twice missed coming to your great country. I have the privilege of having numerous friends there, both known and unknown to me ... I have profited greatly by writings of Thoreau and Emerson. I say this to tell you how much I am connected with your country."

Referring to the grave situation that had prompted him to write to the President, Gandhi told him that "of Great Britain I need say nothing beyond mentioning that in spite of my intense dislike of the British rule, I have numerous friends in England whom I love as dearly as my own people. I had my legal education there. I have therefore nothing but good wishes for your country and Great Britain. You will therefore, accept my word that my present proposal, that the British should unreservedly and without reference to the wishes of the people of India immediately withdraw their rule, is prompted by the friendliest intention. I would like to turn into goodwill the ill will which, whatever may be said to the contrary, exists in India towards Great Britain, and thus enable the millions of India to play their part in the present war ... Under foreign rule, however, we can make no effective contribution of any kind in this war, except as helots."

In order to make his proposal foolproof, Gandhi suggested in his letter that "if the Allies think it necessary, they may keep their troops in India ... for preventing Japanese aggression and defending China," and that the Allied troops will remain in India during the war under treaty with the free India

Government "that may be formed by the people of India without any outside interference, direct or indirect."

Gandhi emphasised in his letter that he held "the full acceptance of my proposal and that only can put the Allied cause on an unassailable basis. I venture to think that the Allied declaration that the Allies are fighting to make the world safe for the freedom of the individual and for the democracy sounds hollow so long as India and for that matter Africa are exploited by Great Britain ... But in order to avoid all complication, in my proposal I have confined myself only to India. If India becomes free, the rest must follow if it does not happen simultaneously ... It is on behalf of this proposal that I write this to enlist your active sympathy."

In his letter to Chiang Kai-shek, Gandhi recalled "five hours of close contact" he had with him earlier that year during Chiang's visit to India, and went on to say that he had "always felt drawn towards you in your fight for freedom, and that contact and our conversation brought China and her problems still nearer to me." He said he had thus "felt greatly attached towards your great country and in common with my countrymen, our sympathy has gone out to you in your terrible struggle."

The letter further stated that "India has been a helpless witness of withdrawals from Malaya, Singapore, and Burma. We must learn the lesson from these tragic events and prevent by all means at our disposal a repetition of what befell these unfortunate countries. But unless we are free we can do nothing to prevent it and the same process might occur again, crippling India and China disastrously. I do not want a repetition of this tragic tale of woe ... ."

"Those of us who would fight for a cause, for India and China, with the armed forces or with non-violence, cannot under the foreign heel function as they want to. And yet our people know for certain that India, free, can play even a decisive part, not only on her behalf, but also on behalf of China and the world for peace ...

"Many like me feel that it is not manly to remain in this helpless state and allow events to overwhelm us when a way of effective action can be opened to us. They feel, therefore, that every possible effort should be made to ensure independence and the freedom of action which is urgently needed. This is the origin of my appeal to British power to end immediately the unnatural connection between British and India ...

"Unless we make that effort, there is grave danger of public feeling in India going into wrong and harmful channels. There is every likelihood of subterranean sympathy for Japan growing simply in order to weaken and oust British authority in India. This feeling may take the place of robust confidence in our ability never to look to outsiders for help in winning our freedom ...

"To make it perfectly clear that we want to prevent in every way Japanese aggression, I would personally agree, and I am sure the Government of free India would agree that the Allied power might under treaty with us, keep their armed forces in India and use the country as a base for operation against the threatened Japanese attack."

* * *

The Congress Working Committee met at Wardha and resolved on July 14 that "the events happening from day to day and the experience the people of India are passing through, confirm the opinion of Congressmen that British rule in India must end immediately, not merely because foreign domination even at its best is an evil in itself ... but because India in bondage can play no effective part in defending herself and in affecting the fortune of the war ..."

The Working Committee drew attention to the fact that "ever since the outbreak of the world war, the Congress had studiedly pursued a policy of non-embarrassment" and that "even at the risk of making its Satyagraha ineffective, it deliberately gave it a symbolic character in the hope that the policy of non-embarrassment ... would be duly appreciated and that real power would be transferred to popular representatives so as to enable the nation to make its fullest contribution towards the realisation of human freedom throughout the world, which is in danger of being crushed."

These hopes, said the Congress, had however been dashed to pieces and the Cripps proposals had shown in the clearest terms that there was no change in the British attitude towards India and that the British hold on India was in no way to be relaxed, even though the Congress in its negotiation with Cripps tried its utmost to achieve the minimum consistent with the national demand. This "has resulted in a rapid and widespread increase of illwill against Britain and a growing satisfaction at the success of Japanese arms."

"The Working Committee view this development with grave apprehension ..." said the resolution. "The Congress would (like to) change the present illwill against Britain into goodwill and make India a willing partner in a joint enterprise of securing freedom for the nations and peoples of the world ... This is possible only if India feels the glow of freedom."

The resolution put on record that "it is the earnest desire of the Congress to enable India to resist aggression effectively with the peoples' united will and strength behind it" and that "in making the proposal for the withdrawal of the British rule from India, the Congress has no desire whatsoever to embarrass Great Britain or Allied Powers in the prosecution of War ... Nor does the Congress intend to jeopardise the defensive capacity of the Allied Powers."

The Congress was therefore agreeable, it stated, to removing any lingering misconception "to stationing of the armed forces of the Allies in India ... in order to ward off and resist Japanese or other aggression and to protect and help China. The proposal of withdrawal of the British power from India was never intended to mean the physical withdrawal of all Britishers from India ... ."

"Should, however, this appeal fail," read the concluding part of the resolution, "the Congress cannot view without the gravest apprehension the continuation of the present state of affairs involving a progressive deterioration in the situation and the weakening of India's will and power to resist aggression. The Congress will then be reluctantly compelled to utilise all the non-violent strength it might have gathered since 1920 ... for the vindication of the political rights and liberty. Such a widespread struggle would inevitably be under the leadership of Mahatma Gandhi."

As the issues involved were of far-reaching consequences, the Working Committee directed the bigger body—All-India Congress Committee—to meet and take a final decision in the matter. The meeting of the AICC was fixed for August 7 in Bombay.

By a telegram the Government of India informed the Secretary of State for India in London that they had come to the conclusion that the Working Committee "resolution as worded does not afford good ground for immediate action against Congress," and that while "it will clearly be desirable to strike before they are ready ... the best moment for doing so may well be immediately after ratification by All-India Congress Committee on August 7" as the terms of the resolution "will necessitate a further interval to allow consideration of appeal by His Majesty's Government with the result that the Congress will not expect to be in a position to launch civil disobedience much before September."[24]

Preparations had however begun to keep Gandhi in detention in the Aga Khan's house at Poona, some of the leaders whose health would not stand long journey somewhere in India, and to fly or take by sea others "for deportation

... using the Arabian route, via Muscat, Aden, Khartoum to Uganda."[25] In a most secret telegram, the Commander-in-Chief, Eastern Fleet, was informing the First Sea Lord in London on July 29 that the "Viceroy has asked for a warship to be at Bombay by August 8th to convoy small number of political prisoners to Kilindini (in Kenya) for Uganda. Intend using H. M. S. Manxman."[26]

In a long and urgent message to President Roosevelt at this point of time Marshal Chiang Kai-shek made yet another attempt to defuse the situation. In his telegram Chiang conveyed to the President that "with both sides remaining adamant in their views, the Indian situation has reached an extremely tense and critical stage." The Chinese believed that the British Government minimised the representative character of the Congress. Granting the existence of Muslims and others, the Chinese believed that the Congress did in fact represent the general Indian aspirations just as for 15 years "the Kuomintang was only an arm of the people but did represent the general Chinese aspirations."

Chiang explained at great length to the President that "the war aims which the anti-aggression nations have proclaimed to the world are two-fold, first to crush brute force and second to secure freedom for all mankind," and that "if India should start a movement against Britain ... the world might entertain doubts as to the sincerity of the lofty war aims of the United Nations."

After analysing the various issues involved and the reasons why the Congress demand should be conceded "for the sake of our common victory," Chiang appealed to Roosevelt that the "United States as the acknowledged leader of democracy has a natural and vital role to play in bringing about a successful solution of the problem ... The war aims of the United Nations and our common interests at stake make it impossible for me to remain silent. An ancient Chinese proverb says: 'Good medicine, though bitter, cures one's illness: words of sincere advice, though unpleasant, should guide one's conduct.' I sincerely hope that Britain will magnanimously and resolutely accept my words of disinterested advice, however unpleasant they may be and believe that they are voiced in the common interest of the United Nations ... I hope Your Excellency will give ... consideration to such practical measures as will break the existing deadlock and avert a crisis ... The United Nations should lose no time in adopting a correct policy towards the Indian situation ... so that our entire war effort will not suffer a major setback."[27]

Roosevelt telegraphed Chiang's message of almost 1,500 words to Churchill with the request to let him have "your thought and any suggestion you may wish to offer with regard to the nature of the reply" that he should send to Chiang.

The reply that Roosevelt received from Churchill was preambled with the classic answer that he had always given to any suggestion for the solution of the Indian problem. "We do not agree with Chiang Kai-shek's estimate of the Indian situation," said Churchill in his telegram. "The Congress Party in no way represents India and is strongly opposed by over 90 million Mohammedans, 40 million untouchables and the Indian states comprising some 90 millions, to whom we are bound by treaty. Congress represents mainly ... nonfighting Hindus."

Churchill's message made it clear that he was going to do nothing about India. "His Majesty's Government here have no intention," he said to Roosevelt, "of making any offer beyond the ... proposals which Sir Stafford Cripps carried to India ... So far as I am concerned I could not accept responsibility for making further proposals at this stage ... I earnestly hope, therefore, Mr. President, that you will do your best to dissuade Chiang Kai-shek from his completely misinformed activities, and will lend no countenance to putting pressure upon His Majesty's Government."[28]

* * *

Soon after the Working Committee adopted its resolution of July 14 at Wardha, Gandhi had sent Mirabehn (daughter of Admiral Sir Edmond Slade of the British Navy, who had joined Gandhi seventeen years earlier) to make his intention abundantly clear and to leave no scope for misunderstanding, to tell the Viceroy that he would do all he could to guide the movement on non-violent lines. For this purpose, however, he must be left free to do so.

Gandhi had, on a previous occasion, called off the mass civil disobedience movement when there had been cases of violence; on this occasion, he informed the Viceroy, he would do his utmost to see that the movement did not deviate from non-violent lines.

The Viceroy had however decided to take pre-emptive steps. "Gandhi and all members of the Working Committee should be simultaneously arrested in Bombay ..." immediately after the AICC had endorsed the Working Committee's resolution, the Government of India informed in its telegram to London on July 24. "Banking on probability that Gandhi will expect an interval after ratification before launching movement ... this action may prevent move from ever taking place."[29]

The secret plan envisaged that as soon as ratification had taken place,

"Bombay Government will inform Government of India, all Provincial Governments, Chief Commissioners and Political Residents by telegram containing prearranged code-word ... Government of India (will) send ... further telegram containing another prearranged code-word which will be the signal for action ... On receipt of telegram from Government of India ... Bombay government will arrest Gandhi and all members of Working Committee who may be in Bombay ... Mahadev Desai, Mirabehn and Dr. Sushila Nayar (lady doctor) will be permitted to accompany Gandhi if they voluntarily accept restrictions on communication which will be imposed on Gandhi himself. If first two refuse to accept these conditions, they will also be arrested ... Lady doctor will not be arrested but will not of course be allowed to attend on Gandhi unless she accepts conditions."[30]

While endorsing the Working Committee's resolution, the AICC directed the Congressmen that if the leaders were removed from the scene suddenly and thus prevented from issuing instructions and guiding the movement, they must remember the general instructions, namely that "non-violence is the basis of this movement."

Addressing the AICC members before the meeting ended well after midnight of August 8, Gandhi told them that "the actual struggle does not commence this very moment. You have merely placed certain powers in my hands. My first act will be to wait upon His Excellency the Viceroy and plead with him for the acceptance of the demand of the Congress. This may take two or three weeks."

The Congress Working Committee was scheduled to meet on the morning of August 9 when Gandhi was to put his views before the Committee regarding the negotiations that he was to carry on with the Government. The instructions about the movement were to issue only on the failure of the contemplated negotiations.

But the Government struck immediately. Within a few hours, before sunrise of August 9, Gandhi and the other leaders were arrested and sent to prison. Gandhi, Sarojini Naidu, Mirabehn, and Gandhi's secretary Mahadev Desai were detained in the desolate Aga Khan's house—called a palace—on the outskirts of Poona. Nehru, Patel, Azad and other Working Committee members arrested in Bombay were taken to Ahmednagar Fort—away from Poona—which was approachable only by a draw-bridge and was surrounded by a moat. Kasturba Gandhi and Dr. Sushila Nayar were later brought in to Aga Khan's palace and detained there with Gandhi. Congress leaders all over the country were arrested and put behind bars.

Gandhi's last instructions conveyed to the nation through his secretary Pyarelal, before he was taken away to prison, were: "Let every non-violent soldier of freedom write out the slogan 'Do or Die' on a piece of paper or cloth, and stick it on his clothes, so that in case he died in the course of satyagraha, he might be distinguished by that sign from other elements who do not subscribe to nonviolence."

"The moment the prison doors closed behind Gandhi," Louis Fischer had recorded, "the sluice gates of violence opened. Police stations and government buildings were set on fire, telegraph lines destroyed, railroad tiles pulled up and British officials assaulted ... Soon a powerful underground movement sprang into existence ... His Majesty's writ no longer ran and his officials no longer appeared in many areas where Indians set up independent village, town and district governments."[31]

Gandhi was allowed no opportunity to launch the contemplated movement and to guide it thereafter on nonviolent lines. He had told Steele of the *New York Herald Tribune* that he would call off the movement if he could be convinced that the British Government could not concede self-rule to India during the war without jeopardising the war effort. He had informed the Viceroy that if he launched the movement, he would do all he could to guide the campaign on non-violent lines but for this purpose he should be allowed to remain free. He had told the AICC delegates in his concluding remarks after midnight of August 8, that they had merely authorised him to launch the movement but the very first step that he would be taking was to meet the Viceroy to plead with him the acceptance of the Congress demand. The Government had admitted that the movement was not expected to be launched much before September in view of further interval necessary for consideration of the Congress appeal by His Majesty's Government. It, however, preferred suppression to discussion and in pursuance of the aim "(a) to avert, (b) to abort and (c) to suppress mass movement" took steps to "prevent the move from ever taking place."[32]

"The facts are: Gandhi never launched the civil disobedience movement ...," noted Louis Fischer. "He had stated that it would not begin until he gave the order ... Had Gandhi remained at liberty he might have prevented... the destruction of property and persons ... he could have curbed the general violence ... The British gained nothing from Gandhi's arrest except the satisfaction... of having him under lock and key ... It deepened the widespread impression that England did not intend to part with power in India."[33]

* * *

The steps that Chiang Kai-shek took on receiving Gandhi's comprehensive and detail letter about the developing Indian political situation have been recorded in earlier pages. We may now focus our attention to the letter that Gandhi sent to the President of the United States of America and the reply that President Roosevelt sent to Gandhi.

Louis Fischer, the American journalist, who had spent a week with Gandhi in his Ashram in June, had offered to deliver Gandhi's letter to Roosevelt in Washington. Writing in *Prologue* (Fall 1969 Issue of the Journal of the National Archives of USA) Mary Walton Livingstone recorded that Louis Fischer who had left Gandhi's Ashram on June 10, was in New Delhi "when Gandhi's letter of July 1 to President Roosevelt reached him. He in turn gave it to Gen. William Gruber, who assured Fischer that he was flying to Washington, and would soon be seeing President Roosevelt. Gruber met the President on July 24 and delivered the letter."

Even as Gandhi's letter was on its way to Washington, events in India were moving towards a climax. On July 14 Congress had adopted its resolution demanding immediate transfer of power by Britain. The resolution envisaged a campaign of mass civil disobedience if independence was not granted.

The large-scale arrests all over India that followed in the second week of August, resulted in disorder breaking out in all parts of the country. President Roosevelt however did not intervene, even though he had received Gandhi's letter by then and Chiang Kai-shek had forcefully pleaded with him to do so as the undisputed leader of the Allied countries.

Roosevelt replied to Gandhi's letter on August 1, 1942. This is what the President wrote in his letter : "My dear Mr. Gandhi: I have received your letter of July 1, 1942, which you have thoughtfully sent me in order that I may better understand your plans, which I well know may have far-reaching effect upon developments important to your country and to mine.

"I am sure that you will agree that the United States has consistently striven for and supported policies of fair dealing, of fair play, and of all related principles looking towards the creation of harmonious relations between nations. Nevertheless, now that war has come as a result of Axis dreams of world conquest, we, together with many other nations, are making a supreme effort to defeat those who would deny forever all hope of freedom throughout the world ... I shall hope that our common interest in democracy and righteousness will enable your countrymen and mine to make common cause against a common enemy."

Roosevelt made no mention in his letter about Indian independence, but sent with the letter a copy of the address of his Secretary of State "made with my complete approval, which illustrates the attitude of this Government."

The address of the US Secretary of State released on July 5, 1942, consisted of five parts containing fifty-seven paragraphs. It appeared in July 25, 1942 issue of the Bulletin of the US Dept of State. It did not deal in anyway with the Indian situation. It referred to the Declaration made one year earlier on August 14, 1941 by President Roosevelt and Prime Minister Churchill, known as Atlantic Charter; the only sentence of which it could be construed to cover India read that "the pledge of the Atlantic Charter is of a system which will give every nation, large or small, a greater assurance of stable peace, greater opportunity for realisation of its aspiration to freedom, and greater facilities for material advancement." Churchill had however soon after announced that Atlantic Charter did not apply to India.

In her article in Prologue Mary Walton Livingston had also noted that in his speech "Gandhi had pledged that he would wait upon the Viceroy and plead with him for the acceptance of the Congress demand. But before any such encounter could take place, British authorities, in the early morning hours of August 9, arrested Gandhi and ... other Congress leaders ... At this stage Roosevelt made no attempt to intervene. He had acknowledged Gandhi's letter ... but he made no mention of Indian independence."

On August 12, Roosevelt ordered US forces in India not to become involved with India's internal affairs. And he informed Churchill that "in view of the message you have sent me, I have replied to Chiang Kai-shek that it does not seem to me to be wise or expedient for the time being to consider taking any of the steps which he suggested in his message to me." Roosevelt however told the Chinese representative at the Pacific Council meeting soon after, that the matter was "nevertheless of general concern to United Nations" and the United Nations must watch the Indian situation "with anxiety."[34]

By the time Roosevelt's reply to Gandhi's letter reached the US Diplomatic Mission in New Delhi, Gandhi along with most of the Congress leaders had been put behind bars. Rather than asking the British authorities to deliver the letter to Gandhi, the Officer incharge of the Mission George Merrell "recommended that it be kept in the confidential files of the office." He cautioned that any approach to the British Government to get the letter delivered would "probably develop the fact that the President's letter" was in reply to one from Gandhi and Government would wonder and perhaps inquire how Gandhi's letter was dispatched from India without passing through censor. He was instructed by the State Department to retain the letter until it could be delivered, and then to ask for instructions.

On Gandhi's release about two years later in May 1944, the Mission in Delhi with Merrell still incharge, asked for and received the instruction that the letter be delivered to Gandhi with the appropriate explanation but with prior advice to the Government. The US Mission then handed the letter to G. D. Birla, the well-known industrialist and a friend of Gandhi, in New Delhi, for passing it on to Mahatma Gandhi. However the letter could not be traced in the records of the Mahatma's papers. A copy of it had to be obtained by the author from Franklin D. Roosevelt Library at Hyde Park, in New York, along with a facsimile copy of Mahatma's letter to the President.

ଔ

3

Prelude to Partition

"I murmured behind the double cordon of an armed guard and the barbed wire isolation of the ... detention camp," recorded Pyarelal in his book *Mahatma Gandhi—The Last Phase*, Gandhi became "the symbol of India's ... unconquerable soul and a beacon of faith and hope to the people."[1]

The British launched a massive propaganda blitz to win American approval for their India policy. Their missions in America and in China were informed in advance about the arrests that were to take place and the repressive measures that were to follow.

"The Government of India, with the approval of His Majesty's Government, have decided that the most vigorous steps must be taken to suppress the movement at the outset," read their telegram to the British Ambassador in Washington, meant for the President of the United States of America. "It is the intention of the Government of India ... promptly to order detention of the leaders, that is of Gandhi and the members of the Working Committee ... The main objective of the action will be to render the movement abortive by removing and detaining its leaders."[2]

The message to Chungking, however, cautioned the British Ambassador to China, that "these intentions are of course strictly secret for the time being, and you should not ... disclose them to General Chiang Kai-shek until after Gandhi and the other Congress leaders have been detained. As soon as you hear that this has been done, you should ... see General Chiang Kai-shek and explain to him ... that our action was taken in the interests of the United Nations as a whole, not merely for protection of British interests in India."[3]

Chiang Kai-shek felt deeply disturbed on learning about the arrests of Gandhi and other leaders. In yet another message to Roosevelt, he expressed his concern at the unfolding events. "I feel certain that you are as concerned as

I am," said Chiang in his telegram," at the news of the arrest of the Working Committee of the Indian Congress including Gandhi and Nehru ... At all costs the United Nations should demonstrate to the world by their action the sincerity of their professed principle of ensuring freedom and justice for men of all races ... I earnestly appeal to you ... to take effective measures ... to solve the pressing problem now facing India."[4]

Chiang told the British Ambassador Sir Horace Seymour that "the pivot of the Indian problem is the Congress. If the problem of the Congress is solved other aspects of the Indian question can be settled without much difficulty."[5]

But Churchill did not consider that "the Congress in any way represents India." Therefore besides serving his standard fare of "90 million Moslems, 40 million untouchables and 90 million in Princely states" whose interest the British could not forgo, and "none of whom are represented by the Congress, which is entirely a Hindu organisation," Churchill said in his telegram in reply to Chiang's message passed on to him by Roosevelt, that he took it amiss "Chiang should seek to make difficulties between us and should interfere in matters ... which affect our sovereign rights. Decision to intern Gandhi was taken by an executive of twelve, at which only one European was present. These Indians are as good Indian patriots and as able men as any of the Congress leaders ... All Chiang's talk of Congress leaders wishing us to quit in order that they may help the Allies is an eyewash. They are concerned with one thing only, namely Congress supremacy ... You could remind Chiang that Gandhi was prepared to negotiate with Japan on the basis of a free passage for Japanese troops through India ..."[6]

This was gross misrepresentation. The facts spoke for themselves. In 1940 while Churchill had been hinting to Roosevelt about "a possible surrender to Nazis by a successor government when his own country was threatened by an invasion," Pyarelal has recorded, Gandhi in 1942 "had been preparing his unarmed countrymen to resist to the last man rather than submit, if the Japanese landed on Indian soil."[7]

In his appeal "to every Japanese," Gandhi had advised them not to fish in troubled waters by invading India and warned that "you will be sadly disillusioned if you believe that you will receive a willing welcome from India ... We will not fail in resisting you with all the might that our country can muster ..."

Replying to a letter that asked how the people should behave in the event of a Japanese landing, Gandhi had said as early as on May 31, 1942, that "our attitude is that of complete non-cooperation with the Japanese army; therefore, we may not help them in any way, nor may we profit by any dealing with them ... If people are not able to face the Japanese army, they will do as the armed soldiers do, i.e. retire when they are overwhelmed ... One thing they should never do—to yield willing submission to the Japanese. That will be a cowardly act, and unworthy of freedom-loving people ... Their attitude therefore must always be of resistance to the Japanese."[8]

And finally, the letters that Gandhi had sent to President Roosevelt and General Chiang Kai-shek in the first week of July 1942, before the Congress adopted the resolution to launch the civil disobedience movement if the British failed to transfer power to the Indians immediately, had left no scope for any misinterpretation or misrepresentation about the intentions of Gandhi or that of the Congress.

Much had been made out too by Churchill in his telegram to Roosevelt about the backing of the Indian members of the Executive Council to the arrest of Gandhi and other leaders. The kind of authority that the Executive Council wielded was clear from what the British Cabinet had itself recorded. The Viceroy must be "in a position to take prompt and decisive action" and should not attach "too great importance to carrying his Executive Council with him in all decisions which have to be taken in this crisis," recorded the British Cabinet. "In the last resort, the responsibility lay with the Viceroy and not with the Council."[9] And while transmitting the Cabinet decision, Amery told Linlithgow that "support of the Indian members of the Council must be forgone" in order to achieve the results.[10]

The Chinese were no doubt a great nuisance if not also suspects. But the Americans were no less. Extraordinary precaution was, therefore, taken to see that no one of any standing in American public life visited India. "I cannot resist the conclusion," wrote the Viceroy to the Secretary of State for India, "... that the Americans are not running entirely straight with us over India. Every one of them of any political eminence who comes through here flirts with the Congress."[11]

Visits to India by Americans even in a private capacity was considered inappropriate. And any political personality was likely openly to express a wish to see Gandhi and the Congress leaders under detention. William Phillips, President Roosevelt's personal envoy in India, was denied permission to meet Gandhi. "I should have liked to meet and talk with Mr. Gandhi," he told press persons. "I requested ... for a permission to do so and I was informed that they were unable to grant the necessary permission." Chiang Kai-shek's innocuous telegram to Gandhi, Nehru and Azad that "I am deeply concerned over your arrest. Please take good care of yourself for your country's sake" was not allowed to be delivered to them.

The Viceroy was directed to make available to the British Mission in Washington, for wide publicity in America, the virulent criticism of the Congress by the Muslim League. In a resolution adopted by it, the Muslim League had recorded that they "are ... firmly convinced that the present Congress movement is ... for the establishment of the Hindu Raj and to deal a death blow to the Muslim goal of Pakistan." The Congress had put forward, it said, "the fantastic theory that the solution of Hindu-Muslim problem can only follow the withdrawal of British power from India," and had added that independence for the Muslim Pakistan and Hindu Hindustan was to follow and not precede acceptance by the Congress of Muslim League demand for the establishment of Muslim homeland of Pakistan.

In a press interview Jinnah expressed his willingness to join the government on a condition that he was given 50 per cent of the seats for the Muslim League and British Government conceded Pakistan.[12] "Jinnah has taken advantage of the latest turn of events," said Linlithgow to Amery in a letter, "to raise his terms against us ... and also to raise them against the Congress.[13]

The British were, however, unable to arrest Gandhi's spirit by putting him in prison or by massive propaganda against him and the Congress. "With the irrepressible ability to take the centre stage," recorded Louis Fischer, "the jailed Mahatma's personality broke through the walls of the Aga Khan's desolate palace and besieged the mind first of the British Government and then of the Indian people."[14]

No sooner had Gandhi arrived in Aga Khan's bungalow than he sent a letter of protest to the Governor of Bombay, Sir Lumley, that while he, Sarojini Naidu, Mirabehn and Mahadev Desai were transported from the railway station to the detention camp in a car, the other leaders brought by the same train were taken to jail in trucks. He felt deeply humiliated. "After the train that carried me and the fellow prisoners reached Chinchwad ... some of us were ordered to alight ... and were directed to get into a car," wrote Gandhi in his letter. "There were two lorries lined up alongside the car. I have no doubt that the reservation of the car for us was done out of delicate considerations ... Nevertheless, I felt deeply humiliated when other fellow prisoners were ordered to occupy the two lorries ... In relating this incident, my object is to inform the government that in the altered conditions and the altered state of my mind, I can no longer accept special privileges which hitherto I have accepted, though reluctantly. I propose this time to accept no privileges and comforts which my comrades may not receive, except for the special food, so long as the government allow it for my bodily need." Finally, he had seen in newspapers on the train "some grossly inaccurate statements" made by the government in justification of its policy, said Gandhi in his letter, "which I ought to be allowed to correct. This ... I cannot do unless I know what is going on outside the jail."

But the British had no intention of allowing Gandhi to know what was happening outside the prison. It had decided in advance that "Gandhi and all members of Working Committee will be precluded absolutely from any form of communication with the outside world."[15]

"There should be a mild but very definite change in our attitude towards Gandhi and his complaint," instructed the Viceroy in his message to the Governor. "It would be ... undersirable that you should send him any message or enter into any communication with him ... The Collector of Poona should inform him personally and orally that his requests for the presence of Vallabhbhai and his daughter and of the Working Committee cannot be acceded to and that it is not ... proposed to let him have newspapers. The Collector should ... refuse to allow himself to be won over by Gandhi's charm ..."[16]

The government was in no position, however, to prevent Gandhi from putting the record straight or from correcting the grossly inaccurate statements made by them. The government "were wrong in precipitating the crisis," wrote Gandhi to the Viceroy within a week of his arrest. "The government resolution justifying this step is full of distortions and misrepresentations. That you have the approval of your Indian 'colleagues' can have no significance except this, that in India you can always command such services ..."

The Government of India should have waited at least till he had written to the Viceroy, Gandhi said in his letter to him. "I had publicly stated that I fully contemplated sending you a letter before taking concrete action ... The Congress has readily filled in every omission that has been discovered in the conception of its demand. So could have I dealt with every difficulty if you had given me the opportunity."

He told the Viceroy that "the precipitate action of the government leads me to think that they were afraid that the extreme caution ... with which the Congress was moving ... might make world opinion veer round to the Congress ... and expose the hollowness of the ground for government's rejection of the Congress demand."

Drawing the attention of the Viceroy to the interesting peroration in the government's resolution which stated that "on them lies the task of defending India, of maintaining India's capacity to wage war, of safeguarding India's interests, of holding the balance between the different sections of the people without fear or favour," the ironies of which were self-evident, Gandhi told the British: "All I can say is that it is a mockery of truth after the experience of Malaya, Singapore and Burma. It is sad to find the Government of India clamouring to hold the 'balance' between the parties for which it is itself demonstrably responsible."

The declared cause was "common between the Government of India and us ...," Gandhi asserted. "It is the protection of the freedom of China and Russia. The Government of India think that the freedom of India is not necessary for winning the cause. I think exactly the opposite. If ... Government's answer to the Congress demand is hasty repression, they will not wonder if I draw the inference that it was not so much the Allied cause that weighed with the British Government, as the unexpressed determination to cling to the possession of India as an indispensable part of the imperial policy."

"It causes me deep pain to have to send you this long letter," wrote Gandhi in conclusion. "But however much I dislike your action I remain the same friend you have known me. I would still plead for reconsideration of the Government of India's whole policy. Do not disregard the pleading of one who claims to be a sincere friend of the British people."

Slamming the door on any further communication or argument for as long as possible, Linlithgow replied to Gandhi in two sentences that he had read his "letter with very close attention... but I fear in the result that it would not be possible for me either to accept the criticisms which you advance of the resolution ... or your request that the whole policy of the Government of India should be reconsidered."

Gandhi and the Congress Working Committee members had been kept "completely isolated and cut off from news." Their places of detention had been kept a secret from the public. No sooner, however, was Gandhi allowed newspapers and learnt of what had happened and was happening than he lost no time in telling the government who in reality was responsible for the violence and destruction that had taken place after the leaders were suddenly prisoned.

"In spite of the chorus of approval sung by the Indian councillors and others of the present government policy in dealing with the Congress," wrote

Gandhi on September 21, not in a letter to the Viceroy but formally to the government, "I venture to assert that ... the Congress policy still remains unequivocally non-violent. The wholesale arrest of the Congress leaders seems to have made the people wild with rage to the point of losing self-control. I feel that the Government, not the Congress, are responsible for the destruction that had taken place."

"Repression can only breed discontent and bitterness," he told the government and advised that "the only right course for the government seems to me to be to release the Congress leaders, withdraw all repressive measures and explore ways and means of conciliation."

Gandhi concluded his letter to the government by saying that since he was now "permitted to receive newspapers, I feel that I owe it to the government to give my reaction to the said happenings in the country. If the government think that as a prisoner I have no right to address such communications, they have but to say so and I will not repeat the mistake."

The government did not wish to concede any such right to Gandhi. Sir Laithwaite, the Viceroy's private secretary, informed India Office in London that "it was not proposed to send Mr. Gandhi a direct reply but the officer-in-charge (of the detention camp) would be instructed to inform him that the Government of India had received his communication."[17]

The British had no intention of responding to reason. They would rather continue with repressive measures. The statements of Prime Minister Churchill and Secretary of State for India Amery in the British Parliament, commented one of the well-known Washington columnists, Ernest Lindley of the *Washington Post*, "confirmed the impression that the British Government's India policy at the present time is solely repressive ..." But since "the Indian problem is no longer or solely British property, or headache" the friendly offices of "the United States or China, or of both probably are necessary ... to explore ... the chances of a provisional settlement ..."[18]

The British had "slammed the door shut against any further attempt at a settlement for the duration of the war" and the Viceroy was opposed to even posting of any high grade American representative in Delhi except on the basis that he would "avoid excursion into ... Indian political field." This notwithstanding the fact that the British Ambassador in Washington, Halifax, had informed the British Government about the widely held view "even in friendly quarters that ... HMG should ... continue to make constructive effort to bring about formation of provisional government, representative of main political parties, during the war" and that "British Government should offer to transfer power to an agreed provisional Indian Cabinet which will, by convention, be allowed to function as such." The Ambassador had cautioned that the American Administration "may not be unwilling to see ... countrywide agitation develop now on these lines."[19]

Gandhi had patience and Gandhi was willing to wait.

* * *

The phrase "Quit India" was neither coined nor used by Gandhi in formulating the Indian demand for independence during the war. The expression he had used was "orderly British withdrawal from India" as against the disorderly withdrawal from Singapore, Malaya and Burma. "My firm opinion is that the British should leave India now in an orderly manner," Gandhi had explained to Horace Alexander, a Quaker friend from England, "and not run the risk that they did in Singapore, Malaya and Burma. That act would mean courage of high order, confession of human limitation and right doing by India ... For they left Burma and Malaya neither to God nor to anarchy, but to the Japanese ... I say 'Don't repeat that story here. Don't leave India to Japan, but leave India to Indians in an orderly manner.'"[20]

Gandhi was clear too about Japanese intentions. "The Japanese may free India from the British yoke," he wrote in *Harijan*, "but only to put in their own instead. I have always maintained that we should not seek any other power's help to free India from the British yoke ..." because "I have no desire to exchange British for any other rule."[21]

He was equally "convinced that the British presence is an incentive for a Japanese attack" and the "presence of the British in India is an invitation to Japan to invade India."[22]

But if the British conceded self-rule to India and a National Government took over, the situation would get radically altered. The very first act of the National Government, wrote Gandhi in *Harijan* of June 14, 1942, "would be to enter into a treaty with the United Nations for defensive operations against aggressive powers, it being common case that India will have nothing to do with any of the Fascist Powers and India would be morally bound to help the United Nations."

The British were, however, more afraid of losing India to Indians than to the Japanese.

Even though Gandhi's stand was open and clear, and in answer to Churchill's request to provide him with "a note on Mr. Gandhi's intrigues with Japan," Amery had replied that "the India office has no evidence to show, or to suggest, that Gandhi had intrigued with Japan,"[23] Gandhi continued to be "vilified in the world Press by the ... British propaganda as pro-Japanese and denied the elementary right to defend himself ..."[24]

After waiting for several months Gandhi, therefore, took the decision that the only way left to make his protest public against the false propaganda and the repressive measures was for him to use the ultimate weapon available to a non-violent soldier when all other weapons had failed.

In a personal letter to the Viceroy on the New Year Eve of 1942, Gandhi told him that he did not wish the old year to end "without disburdening myself of what is rankling in my breast against you. I had thought we were friends ... However what has happened since 9th of August last makes me wonder whether you still regard me as a friend."

Gandhi explained why he thought so. "Your arrest of me, the communique you issued thereafter, Mr. Amery's attack on me and much else I can catalogue to show that at some stage or other you must have suspected my bonafides ..."

If the Viceroy still considered him a friend, said Gandhi, "why did you not, before taking drastic action, send for me, tell me your suspicions and made yourself sure of your facts. I am quite capable of seeing myself as others see me but in this case I have failed hopelessly."

He found, Gandhi wrote in his letter, that "all the statements made about me in government quarters ... contain palpable departure from truth" and yet he was "expected to condemn the so-called violence ... although I have no data for such condemnation save the heavily censored reports of newspapers."

He had partaken the comforts provided to him in the detention camp, said Gandhi concluding his letter, "in the hope that some day those that have the power will realise that they have wronged innocent men. I had given myself six months. The period is drawing to a close, so is my patience. The law of Satyagraha ... prescribes a remedy in such moments of trial. In a sentence it is to 'crucify the flesh by fasting.' The same law forbids its use except as a last resort. I do not want to use it if I can avoid it. This is the way to avoid it: convince me of my error or errors and I shall make ample amends."

A few weeks earlier when Gandhi sent to the Viceroy a letter of condolence for Lord Halifax saying that he had read about the sad but heroic death of Peter Wood, his son, in action and wanted to convey to him "my congratulations as well as condolences on the sad bereavement," the Viceroy had sent Gandhi's letter to Amery for transmission to Halifax with the comment that the letter was "characteristic of the Mahatma in more ways than one."[25]

But Gandhi's letter now to "convince me of my error ... and I shall make ample amends" and to that end "you can send for me or send someone who knows your mind and can carry conviction" produced altogether a different reaction in Linlithgow.

It would be unwise "to hurry or to show any particular concern at Gandhi's move," said the Viceroy in his telegram to Amery on receipt of Gandhi's letter. And in his reply sent to Gandhi a fortnight later on January 13, the Viceroy said that when arrangements were made that he and the Working Committee should have such newspapers as they desired in prison, "I felt certain that the detail these newspapers contained ... would shock and distress you ... and that you would be anxious to make your condemnation of it categorical and widely known. But that was not the case; and it has been a real disappointment to me ... ."

It was not necessary for the Viceroy to convince Gandhi of his errors for which he and the Congress Working Committee had been detained. But if in the light of what had happened, "you wish now to retrace your steps and dissociate yourself from the policy" that he and the Congress had followed, "you have only to let me know and I will at once consider the matter further."

The correspondence with the Viceroy proved a futile exercise. "I wanted to fast and should still want to if nothing comes out of our correspondence and I have to be a helpless witness to what is going on in the country," wrote back Gandhi. But if he could be convinced of his "error or worse ... I should need to consult nobody, so far as my own action is concerned, to make a full and open confession and make ample amends ..." He could not express any opinion on events which he could not influence or control and of which he had but one-sided account. In the past he had condemned openly and unequivocally any violence on the part of the Congress workers. But on every such occasion he did it as a free man.

If the Viceroy, therefore, wanted him to act on his own, said Gandhi, he should convince him that he was wrong; and if he wanted him to speak on behalf of the Congress, he should put him among the Congress Working Committee. "I do plead with you to make up your mind to end the impasse ... I have no mental reservation."

The Viceroy said in his reply of January 25 that he had made it clear to Gandhi in his earlier letter "that ... the course of events ... has left me no choice but to regard the Congress movement and you as its authorised and fully empowered spokesman ... as responsible for the sad campaign of violence and crime ..."

Gandhi held his ground. "You should at least make an attempt to convince me of the validity of the opinion you hold," replied Gandhi, that the August resolution of the Congress was responsible for the violence, even though it broke out after the wholesale arrest of Congressmen. "Surely I can say with safety that it is for the government to justify this action by solid evidence."

"If then I cannot get a soothing balm for my pain," said Gandhi in conclusion, "I must resort to the law prescribed for Satyagrahis, namely a fast according to capacity. I must commence ... a fast for 21 days ... My wish is not to fast unto death, but to survive the ordeal, if God so wills." The Viceroy promptly replied that while he greatly regretted Gandhi's decision to go on fast, he saw in his decision an attempt "to find an easy way out" and regarded the "use of fast for political purpose as a form of political blackmail."

Replying in his final letter on February 7, 1943, Gandhi told the Viceroy that his letter, "from a Satyagrahi's standpoint, is an invitation to fast ... That you, as a friend, can impute such a base and cowardly motive to me passes comprehension ..." It left him no loophole for "escaping the ordeal I have set before myself ... Despite your description of it as 'a form of political blackmail,' it is on my part meant to be an appeal to the Highest Tribunal for justice which I have failed to secure from you. If I do not survive the ordeal, I shall go to the Judgement Seat with the fullest faith in my innocence. Posterity will judge between you as a representative of an all-powerful government and me as a humble man who has tried to serve his country and humanity through it."

Even before Gandhi was detained, the government had decided that "if unfortunately Gandhi fasts, 'cat and mouse' procedure will be followed ... He will be given every facility to take food and receive constant medical attention but will be released as soon as his life is in danger to avoid possibility of his death as a prisoner."[26]

The British Cabinet did not agree to this arrangement. It directed that "the Government of India should ... take a firm decision ... that if Gandhi fasted while in detention, the 'cat and mouse' procedure would not in any circumstances be applied, and that Gandhi must continue in detention whatever the consequences."[27]

The Viceroy's own views had always been that "Gandhi should be allowed to fast to death" and he was likely to insist on "starving himself to death in the Aga Khan's Palace."[28] The news that Gandhi had no intention to fast to death but to survive the ordeal of 21 days' fast, therefore, came to him as a disappointment. The government, however, decided to release him for the purpose and for the duration of the fast. Gandhi refused to avail of this concession. "If the temporary release is offered for my convenience, I do not need it," he informed the government. "The impending fast has not been conceived to be undertaken as a free man ... If therefore I am released, there will be no fast ... I shall have to survey the situation de novo and decide what I should do."[29]

Medical opinion was firm that Gandhi could not survive for more than a few days.

The Governor of Bombay in his telegram to the Viceroy warned that "Gandhi's death in detention would do great permanent damage to Indian sentiment ... and would do unreparable damage to British Indian relation."[30] Three members of the Viceroy's Executive—Aney, Mody and Sarkar—resigned on the ground that "the majority decision not to release Gandhi unconditionally even when danger to his life accrued from the fast ... is one which we cannot possibly support."[31]

The message from Cordell Hull, the American Foreign Secretary, and Roosevelt, expressing their "deep concern over the political crisis in India" and to express the "hope that means may be discovered to avoid the deterioration of the situation which would be almost certain to occur if Gandhi dies"[32] was ignored. Similar advice from General Smuts of South Africa and the Australian Prime Minister was also explained away.

While Gandhi's condition deteriorated, Churchill inquired from the Viceroy that he had "heard that Gandhi usually has glucose in his water when doing his various fasting antics" and wanted Linlithgow to verify the fact. He received the reply that the "present Surgeon-General Bombay (a European) says that in a previous fast Gandhi was particularly careful to guard against possibility of glucose being used. I am told that his present medical attendants tried to persuade him to take glucose yesterday and again today, and that he refused absolutely."[33]

* * *

All the information about Gandhi's fast available with him, and all relating official documents at his disposal, could not come however in the way of Churchill from recording the following in his memoir of the Second World War that appeared in 1951, four years after the passing away of Gandhi.

"Early in February (1943) Mr. Gandhi announced he would fast for three weeks. He was in detention ... in a small palace at Poona, watched with ceaseless vigilance both by British and his own Indian doctors. He continued obdurately to fast and most active worldwide propaganda was set on foot that his death was approaching. It was certain however at an early stage that he was being fed with glucose whenever he drank water ... In the end, being quite convinced of our obduracy, he abandoned his fast and his health ... was not seriously affected. The incident was one which caused much anxiety because Mr. Gandhi's death would have produced a profound impression throughout India ... We however had judged the situation rightly."

Gandhi had neither taken glucose with water during his fast, nor "abandoned the fast" convinced of British obduracy. The present author brought Churchill's statement in his memoir to the notice of Pyarelal, Gandhi's secretary, and his sister Dr. Sushila Nayar, both of whom had been co-prisoners with Gandhi in the detention camp in Poona. I was assisting Pyarelal at the time on his biography project of Gandhi. It led to a joint letter sent to Churchill under the signatures of Dr. B. C. Roy, Dr. Gilder, Dr. Sushila Nayar and Pyarelal. The three doctors named had looked after Gandhi during his fast. No response came to the communication and a reminder had to be sent after due interval, which brought a brief reply from Churchill's secretary informing on his behalf that appropriate correction would be made when the book went for reprint. No regret was however expressed for making the damaging statement even many years after Gandhi's passing away.

* * *

The British had concluded that Gandhi would certainly die before completing the fast. Surgeon-General "Candy is now of the opinion ...," read Linlithgow's telegram to Amery of February 15, 1943, "that Gandhi cannot manage to last 21 days." Two days later, "General Candy and Colonels Bhandari and Shah report tonight" that Gandhi's "general condition is serious" and "Candy's estimate is that collapse might come any time." Preparations were made accordingly. It was arranged that "Bombay Government will send ... a most immediate *en clair* telegram" to all concerned containing the code word "RUBICON" if death occurs. At the same time "Bombay Government will arrange to stop all trunk telephone calls and telegrams ... from Poona and neighbourhood ... after despatch of "RUBICON" telegram ... Considering Gandhi's position as our prisoner and a rebel, there can be no question of half-masting flags or sending official message of condolence to his widow."[34]

The government considered this as the most appropriate time, too, to publish its infamous booklet to slander Gandhi and the Congress, as the Mahatma on all account was dying.

But Gandhi survived. Churchill's reaction was that "it now seems almost certain that the old rascal will emerge all the better from his so-called fast."[35]

Gandhi's imprisonment, observed Bernard Shaw, had "wiped out our moral case against Hitler. The King should release Mr. Gandhi immediately as an act of grace unconnected with policy and apologise to him for the mental defectiveness of his Cabinet."[36]

"Churchill fought the Second World War to preserve the heritage of Britain," wrote Louis Fischer. "Churchill regarded India as Britain's property ... From the time he became the King's First Minister in 1940 to the day he went out of office in 1945, Churchill was in conflict with Gandhi. It was a contest between the past of England and the future of India."[37]

As soon as Gandhi recovered from his 21-days ordeal, he requested the government to make available to him a copy of the offending publication, *Congress Responsibility for Disturbances*. The government took more than a month to do so. It contained several corrections made in red ink.

In a letter to the government, running into seventyseven paragraphs, Gandhi made mincemeat of the charges levelled against him and the Congress. "I take it that the government have based the charges made in the publication against the Congress and myself on the material printed therein and not on the evidence which, as stated in the preface, is withheld from the public," said Gandhi in his letter.

"The Preface is dated 13th February ... that is, three days after the commencement of my recent fast. The date is ominous," wrote Gandhi questioning the intention of the government. "Why was the period of my fast chosen for publishing a document in which I am the target?"

"The preface commences thus: 'In response to demands which have reached the Government from several sources, the Government have now prepared a review which brings together a number of facts ... bearing on the responsibility of Mr. Gandhi and of the Congress High Command for the disturbances which followed the sanctioning of a mass movement by the All-India Congress Committee on August 8, 1942.'

"There is an obvious misstatement here. The disturbances followed not the 'sanctioning of the mass movement by the AICC' but the arrests made by the government. As for the 'demands,' so far as I am aware, they began soon after the wholesale arrests of the principal Congressmen all over India. As the government are aware, in my letters to the Viceroy, the last being dated the 7th February 1943, I had asked for proof in support of my alleged guilt. The evidence now produced might have been given to me when I raised the question. Had my request been complied with, one advantage would certainly have occurred. I would have been heard in answer to the charges brought against me. That very process would have delayed the fast, and who knows, if government had been patient with me, it might have even prevented it.

"The preface contains the following sentence: 'Almost all the facts presented in this review are, or should be, already within the knowledge of the public.' Therefore, so far as the public are concerned, there was no such hurry as to require publication of the document during the fast. This train of reasoning has led me to the inference that it was published in expectation of my death which medical opinion must have considered almost a certainty. It was feared even during my previous long fasts. I hope my inference is wholly wrong and the government had a just and valid reason for choosing the time that they did, for the publication of what is after all an indictment of the Congress and me. I hope to be pardoned for putting on paper an inference, which if true, must discredit the government. I feel that I am being just to them by unburdening myself of a suspicion instead of harbouring it and allowing it to cloud my judgement about their dealings with me.

"I now come to the indictment itself. It reads like a presentation of his case by a prosecutor. In the present case the prosecutor happens to be also the policeman and jailor. He first arrests and gags his victims, and then opens his case behind their backs.

"I have read it again. I have gone through the numbers of *Harijan* which my companions happened to have with them, and I have come to the conclusion that there is nothing in my writings and my doings that could have warranted the inferences and the innuendoes of which the indictment is full. In spite of my desire to see myself in my writings as the author has seen me, I have failed completely.

"The indictment opens with a misrepresentation. I am said to have deplored 'the introduction of foreign soldiers into India to aid in India's defence.' In *Harijan* article on which the charge is based, I have refused to believe that India was to be defended through the introduction of foreign soldiers. If it is India's defence that is aimed at, why should trained Indian soldiers be sent away from India and foreign soldiers brought in instead? Why should the Congress—an organisation which was born and lives for the very sake of India's freedom—be suppressed? I am clearer today in my mind than I was when I penned that article on April 16th, that India is not being defended, and that if things continue to shape themselves as they are, she will sink at the end of war deeper than she is today, so that she might forget the very word freedom."

With all the above information in official records of the Government, Churchill had no problem in stating in his memoir that "the Congress party committed themselves to an aggressive policy taking the form of sabotage of railways and fermenting riots and disorder."

Within a few months of the fast, the Viceroy was returning to England at the end of his term. Gandhi sent him a brief note, on September 27, 1943, from the detention camp which read: "Dear Lord Linlithgow, On the eve of your departure from India I would like to send you a word. Of all the high functionaries I have had the honour of knowing, none have been the cause of such deep sorrow to me as you have been. It has cut me to the quick to have to think of you as having countenanced untruth and that regarding one whom you at one time considered your friend. I hope and pray that God will some day put in into your heart to realise that you, a representative of a great nation, have been led into a grievous error. With good wishes, I still remain your friend, M. K. Gandhi."

* * *

On a visit to Inverness in northern Scotland almost half a century later, my train from Edinbrough stopped at a small railroad station. No one got down, no one boarded the train there. When out of curiosity I looked out for the signboard of the station, it read: Linlithgow. This is all that has remained perhaps to remember him in a far corner of Scotland. Posterity had by then given its judgement between him as an arrogant "representative of an all-powerful Government" and Gandhi as "a humble man who tried to serve his country and humanity through it."

* * *

In less than a week of their arrival in the detention camp in August 1942, Gandhi had lost Mahadev Desai. Kasturba, who was keeping indifferent health, fell seriously ill in December 1943 and, two months later, passed away in February 1944. "Two of his closest comrades—his devoted secretary for twenty-five years ... and ... his wife ..." recorded Pyarelal in his book, "were cremated under his very eyes in the shadow of the detention camp." This did not however cause Gandhi to waver or lose faith. He stood firm "without a trace of bitterness or doubt or despair, and continued to bear witness to the justice and innocence of his stand ... ."[38] And on finding no change in the government's attitude even with the change of the Viceroy, he wrote to Lord Wavell, the successor to Linlithgow, on April 9, 1944, that "whilst you hold the views expressed in your letter ... the proper place for one like me is ... prison. And unless there is a change of heart, view and policy on the part of the government, I am quite content to remain your prisoner."

About this time Gandhi himself suffered "a severe attack of benign tertian malaria, during which he was delirious. His temperature rose to 105 degrees." Bombay Government informed Amery on April 28 that "medical opinion is that he stands risk of getting an attack of coronary thrombosis. His general condition is weak ..." The Government considered shifting him to Ahmednagar Fort because "Ahmednagar is free from malaria" and it was important that "he should not stay in a place where he is likely to get malaria again."[39]

Subsequent medical report showed "progressive deterioration in Gandhi's anaemia, blood pressure and kidney functions all of which in the opinion of ... Surgeon General Candy have tendency to produce coronary or cerebral thrombosis" and in Candy's words "he is on the slippery slope." The government now did not want Gandhi to die in detention. It decided to release him unconditionally on May 6, 1944, "on medical grounds."[40]

* * *

Two attempts were made by the British, after failure of the Cripps Mission in 1942, to form a National government representing political parties: First in the summer of 1945 by Lord Wavell, and then in the summer of 1946 by the Cabinet Delegation sent to India after Attlee had become Prime Minister of Great Britain. But by then the situation had also become far too complicated, and the veto given to the minority community by the British had come home to roost.

In June 1945 Wavell announced that he would attempt at forming a National government with equal number of caste-Hindus and Muslims in consultation with the political parties. He simultaneously released the Congress leaders from detention.

The introduction of "caste-Hindu Muslim parity" in the government to be formed was indicative of the shape of things to come. "Personally I can never subscribe to it, nor the Congress, if I know its mind," Gandhi had wired to the Viceroy in answer to his invitation to attend the meeting convened by him for the purpose. "In spite of overwhelming Hindu membership, the Congress has striven to be purely political. I am quite capable of advising the Congress to nominate all non-Hindus and most decidedly non-caste Hindus."

"Unfortunately, the Congress Working Committee could not be persuaded to adopt Gandhiji's proposal," Pyarelal had recorded.[41] Even so, the Viceroy failed in his endeavour because Jinnah, the Muslim League President, demanded an assurance that all Muslim members of the Government would be selected by the Viceroy from the Muslim League alone.

Mukul Kesavan, who attended on Jinnah at the time in the hotel at Simla, has recorded the conversation he had heard on the eve of the Viceroy's conference, about the strategy that the Muslim League was to follow at the meeting. "The British owned this country," Jinnah told his colleagues who were to attend the conference with him, "not the Congress. The Congress can give us nothing. Ignore it. The British can but they won't until they are forced to. We are too small to force them to do what we want, but big enough to veto anything that does not suit us."[42]

The net result of the conference called by the Viceroy for the formation of the government, recorded Pyarelal in his book, "was to introduce the formula of caste-Hindu Muslim parity into practical politics and stereotype officially the principle of religious division on the eve of independence."[43]

In March 1946, the British Cabinet sent three of its members to negotiate with the Indian leaders formation of a National Government as well as to formulate with them the principles for working out a Constitution. Gandhi expressed the hope that "what was being promised to the ear would not be broken to the hope" by the British this time.[44]

Pyarelal has recorded Gandhi's conversation with a staff member of the Cabinet Delegation. "Do you think we are getting off your back?" Woodrow Wyatt asked Gandhi.

"I feel you will," replied Gandhi. "But you must have the strength."

"Supposing we imposed what we considered to be a just solution and went?"

"All would be upset."

"So it must be left to India's decision?"

"Yes, leave it to the Congress and the League ... I will advise you to try him (Jinnah) and if you feel he cannot deliver the goods, take the Congress into your confidence."[45]

The Cabinet Delegation failed to bring the Congress and the Muslim League to an agreement. It then announced its own recommendations to ensure a speedy setting up of a constitution-making body and for the formation of an Interim Government having the support of major political parties.

Gandhi considered the announcement as "the best document the British Government could have produced in the circumstances." He recorded in *Harijan* that his compliment, however, did "not mean that what is best from the British standpoint is also best or even good from the Indian. Their best may possibly be harmful ..."[46]

The document of the Cabinet Delegation was a complicated one. The Congress interpreted the document in one way, the Muslim League in another—that it contained the seed of Pakistan—and the Cabinet Delegation in a third way—that it had rejected a separate Pakistan but had conceded the substance of it! Even so, the Cabinet Delegation allowed itself to believe that both the Congress and the Muslim League accepted their constitution-making proposals, and proceeded to negotiate the formation of the Interim Government. But they found themselves facing the same hurdle that had wrecked Lord Wavell's attempts a year earlier. On the failure of the Congress and the Muslim League to come to an agreement, the Cabinet Delegation announced the names of those who might join the Interim Government on the basis of parity between caste-Hindus and Muslims. The Congress would not agree to it because it was not allowed to nominate even a nationalist Muslim as one of its representatives in the government; Jinnah would not agree because all the Muslim seats were not offered to the Muslim League.

Expressing satisfaction, however, that both the Congress and the Muslim League had accepted their proposals for the constitution-making body, and after announcing that the Viceroy would make a fresh attempt at forming the Interim Government, the Cabinet Delegation left for England after spending three months in India.

He had no distrust of the Cabinet Mission or the Viceroy, Gandhi explained to Norman Cliff of the *News Chronicle*, London, but he had distrust of "the way things have gone." The Cabinet Delegation had admitted, said Gandhi, that the "ideal course to follow was the democratic principle of handing over power to one or the other party." They had also agreed "in principle" that if they could not trust the League they should put trust squarely on the shoulders of the Congress and rely upon it to do the right thing by India as a whole. But they must try, the British felt, "for the cooperation of both sides." They therefore followed not the best or ideal course but the second best because, in their opinion, "the theoretically best is not practical."[47]

To Gandhi the British "concern for the minorities was a relic of imperialism," Pyarelal had recorded, "which the British could not shake off ... They had to discard it and dare to do the right" even though it might displease some.[48]

"What happens after the British leave?" Woodrow Wyatt had asked Gandhi, if the British accepted his advice? "Probably there will be arbitration ... But there might be a blood-bath," Gandhi had replied. "It will be settled in two days ... if I can persuade India to go my way, or the ordeal may last longer ... If the Congress can come to terms with the League, there will be no difficulty." But if Jinnah chose otherwise, "Congress and you must not be frightened."[49]

4

Gandhi and Partition

Mahatma Gandhi considered division of India by the British a disaster. Jinnah's hand in partition was obvious. What was, however, not so obvious to the public eye was the part that the Congress leaders and the Viceroy had played in this great tragedy.

Gandhi had remained uncompromising till the last in his opposition to the partition of India in any shape or form by the British. With his characteristic foresight he had warned the nation about the disaster and ruin the country would have to face, and the bitterness and animosity that partition would leave behind in its trail, if they allowed the British to divide India on communal lines before handing over the power. He had repeatedly advised the British to do the right with India and leave India even to chaos.

The curtain on the drama leading to partition of India had been rolled up by the Congress when abandoning its age-long stand against division of the country, on communal or religious lines, it demanded a few weeks before the arrival of the last Viceroy in March 1947, partition of the Punjab into Hindu and Muslim majority areas without consulting Gandhi. Pyarelal, Gandhi's secretary, lamented in his biography of the Mahatma that "such a thing would have been inconceivable" earlier and that the Congress leadership had never failed to consult Gandhi before taking any vital decision in the past.[1]

Only a few weeks earlier Nehru had written to Gandhi that "we are drifting everywhere and sometimes I doubt if we are drifting in the right direction."[2] On reading the Congress resolution about the Punjab Gandhi felt all the more necessary to ask Nehru to tell him the reason and background behind the Congress decision "on the possible partition of the Punjab." In reply Nehru wrote that he felt convinced that "we must press for the immediate division (of Punjab) so that reality might be brought into the picture. Indeed this is the only answer to the partition as demanded by Jinnah."[3] And to Gandhi's request "to explain to me your Punjab resolution if you can," Sardar Patel had replied that "it is difficult to explain to you the resolution about the Punjab ... Nothing has been done in a hurry."[4]

Gandhi saw the slippery ground over which the Congress leadership had stepped on. Nehru's letter made it clear that the Congress was now prepared to barter the unity of the country on its own terms as against the terms of Jinnah. The decision of the Congress, however, made Gandhi only more determined to wage a last-ditch fight to prevent the country from the unmitigated disaster of division at British hands.

Within a fortnight of Mountbatten's arrival in Delhi in March 1947 as the last Viceroy, Gandhi urged him at their very first meeting, as he had been repeatedly advising the British earlier, "to have the courage to see the truth and act by it even though the correct solution might mean grievous loss of life ... on an unprecedented scale" after the British departure.[5] He presented in writing a couple of days later the outlines of the scheme that he had discussed with an astonished Viceroy earlier as the solution of the Indian problem that he wanted Mountbatten to adopt to prevent partition of the country before transfer of power and British withdrawal by June 1948. The outlines of Gandhi's proposal were: Jinnah to be given the option of forming a Cabinet. The selection of the Cabinet to be left entirely to Jinnah.

If Jinnah accepted this offer, the Congress would guarantee to cooperate freely and sincerely so long as all measures that Jinnah's Cabinet bring forward were in the interests of the Indian people as a whole.

The sole referee of what was or was not in the interest of India as a whole would be Lord Mountbatten in his personal capacity.

Jinnah must stipulate on behalf of the Muslim League or any other parties represented in the Cabinet formed by him that so far as he or they were concerned, they would do their utmost to preserve peace throughout India.

There shall be no National Guards or any other form of private army.

Within the above framework Jinnah will be perfectly free to present for acceptance a scheme of Pakistan even before transfer of power, provided however that he was successful in his appeal to reason and not to the force of arms, which he abjures for all time for this purpose. Thus there will be no compulsion in this matter over a Province or a part thereof.

In the Assembly the Congress has a decisive majority. But the Congress shall never use that majority against the League policy simply because of its identification with the League but will give its hearty support to every measure brought forward by the League Government, provided that it is in the interest of the whole of India. Whether it is in such interest or not shall be decided by Lord Mountbatten as a man and not in his representative capacity.

If Jinnah rejects this offer, the same offer to be made, with due alterations of details, to the Congress.

"If you are not to leave a legacy of chaos behind," Gandhi advised the Viceroy, "you have to make your choice and leave the government of the whole of India ... to one party." He had given similar advice to Stafford Cripps in 1942 and to Viceroy Lord Wavell in 1946, when attempts had been made to end the political deadlock by bringing in the political parties into the government.

The Viceroy told Gandhi that "your plan has many attractions for me"[6] but it would require "an assurance from some of the other leaders that they considered it capable of being implemented" before he could commit himself to support it.[7]

The Viceroy had also recorded that before taking any step on Gandhi's plan, "he must first be convinced that Pandit Nehru agreed with it."[8] Gandhi, in turn, had informed Mountbatten that those leaders of the Congress he had spoken to had all agreed that his plan was workable. However, Gandhi had added, Nehru had at least one vital "objection" to the plan but that he would "discuss Pandit Nehru's objection" later with the Viceroy, if the outline given by him appeared workable to Mountbatten.[9]

Mountbatten had further recorded that the two leaders with whom he discussed Gandhi's plan, Maulana Azad "staggered me by saying that in his opinion" Gandhi's plan "was perfectly feasible of being carried out, since Gandhi could unquestionably influence the Congress to accept it, and work it loyally." And on asking Khan Abdul Ghaffar Khan "if he really thought the Congress would accept this scheme and that it would be workable," he gave "a very definite affirmative reply."[10]

The Viceroy had recorded too that Gandhi "volunteered to place his whole service at my disposal in trying to get the Jinnah Government through first by exercising his influence with the Congress to accept it, and secondly by touring the length and breadth of the country getting all the people of India to accept the decision. He convinced me of his sincerity."[11]

Mountbatten told his advisers about "Mr. Gandhi's amazing personal influence which might induce Congress to accept" his plan and that "it would not be very easy for Mr. Jinnah to refuse Mr. Gandhi's offer." The assessment that he gave to his advisers was that "basically, Mr. Gandhi's object was to retain the unity of India" and that "Mr. Gandhi honestly felt ... that Muslims' fear must be removed before it could be made to work better. Once the British had handed over to a unified India, Mr. Gandhi doubtless thought that the Indians themselves would be able to adjust matters and set up some sort of Pakistan if necessary."[12]

The Viceroy had also noted that "Mr. Gandhi's viewpoint was that since it was impossible to get Mr. Jinnah to agree to the Congress running the Interim Government, the only way was to get Mr. Jinnah to run it himself and for him (Mr. Gandhi) to use his great influence to induce Congress to accept that."[13]

On finding that "Mr. Jinnah was determined to have Pakistan, and Congress, with the exception of Mr. Gandhi, appeared to let him have it,"[14] the Viceroy told Jinnah that he "regarded it as a very great tragedy" that Jinnah should be trying to force him "to give up the idea of a united India," and that if he accepted Jinnah's arguments in the case of India as a whole, he had to apply the same logic in the case of Punjab and Bengal since he "could not visualise being so inconsistent as to agree to the partition of India without also agreeing to partition within any provinces in which the same problem arose."[15]

In answer to Jinnah's argument that "cutting out half of Punjab and Bengal, including Calcutta" would make Pakistan "economically very difficult if not impossible to function," the Viceroy had told Jinnah that the "moth-eaten Pakistan ... was all I could possibly offer him" and that if he insisted on partition, he would have thrown away the substance for the shadow, and that he was going to get an almost unworkable, truncated Pakistan."[16]

While recording that "until he had met Mr Jinnah, he had not thought it possible that a man with such a complete lack of sense of responsibility could hold the power which he did," the Viceroy noted that Jinnah was "intent on his Pakistan—which could surely only result in doing the Muslims irreparable damage"[17] as a very large Muslim population would still have to stay behind on the other side of the divided country.

Mountbatten had also recorded that Jinnah was "most distressed at the way my mind was working" and appealed to him "not to destroy the unity of Bengal and the Punjab which has national characteristic in common; common history, common ways of life; and where Hindus have stronger feelings as Bengalis or Punjabis than they have as members of the Congress."[18]

The Viceroy told Jinnah that "it was a day-dream" of his (Mountbatten's) "to be able to put the Central Government under the Prime Ministership of Mr. Jinnah himself"[19] and later related to his advisers that his "tentative suggestion to Mr. Jinnah that he might become Prime Minister had a far greater effect on Mr. Jinnah than he would have thought possible."[20]

The situation was thus tailor-made to implement Gandhi's scheme to avoid partition of the country by the British. That stage however never arrived. The officials felt uneasy. It is interesting to note the way they reacted to the solution offered by Gandhi.

Speaking for them in the staff meeting, Ismay, the Viceroy's Chief of Staff, told Mountbatten that he himself, Eric Mieville, George Abell and V. P. Menon, the Reforms Commissioner, had all "come to a unanimous conclusion that Mr. Gandhi's scheme was not workable," and that the scheme was not a new scheme. The Viceroy thereupon told his advisers that "Mr Gandhi had made no attempt to disguise" the fact that his proposed scheme was not a new one. But the new situation made the implementation of the old scheme essential.

Eric Mieville wanted to know "what influence Mr. Gandhi had with the rank and file of the Congress party" to which George Abell replied that "Mr. Gandhi's influence with the rank and file of the Congress party was considerable, but he had more difficulty with the leaders, particularly Sardar Patel."[21]

V. P. Menon mentioned that "since the Cabinet Delegation's visit ... Gandhi is out of accord with the policy of the Congress Working Committee as well as members of the Interim Government on several questions of major importance. It should not, therefore, be taken for granted that his present proposals will carry the support of either the Congress Working Committee or of Nehru and Patel."[22]

The possibility of the Congress Working Committee passing a resolution to support Gandhi's proposals made the Viceroy's advisers jittery. They were able to prevail upon the Viceroy that "it was essential to make clear to Nehru before Gandhi gets to work too hard upon the Congress that Mountbatten was far from committed to Gandhi Plan."[23]

Nehru was made aware that before acting on Gandhi's plan, the Viceroy wanted to be sure that Nehru, not necessarily the Congress Working Committee, supported the Gandhi plan.

Mountbatten discussed with Nehru the very next day of his meeting with Gandhi the plan that Gandhi had outlined to him orally. He was "not surprised to hear of the solution," said Nehru to the Viceroy, "since this was the same solution that Mr. Gandhi had put up to the Cabinet Mission. It was turned down then as being quite impracticable." And the bloodshed and the bitterness that had taken place since then, Nehru added, "made the solution even less realistic now than a year ago."[24]

To cut the long and arduous story short, Nehru told Gandhi at the end of a series of meetings with him, that "he saw many difficulties in the plan" which he had outlined to the Viceroy and was therefore not in a position to support it.[25]

Gandhi had tried to convince Nehru that the only way left to preserve the unity of the country at that stage was for the Congress to back his scheme and come out of the government. It was then for the Viceroy to persuade Jinnah to give the scheme an honest trial, which the Viceroy had offered to do if the scheme had the backing of Nehru.

On finding that he had failed to persuade Nehru, Gandhi with a heavy heart decided to withdraw himself from the negotiations with the Viceroy, notwithstanding the fact that all those of the Congress leaders Gandhi had spoken to about the plan, had agreed that his plan was workable. There was thus no occasion for Gandhi to discuss with the Viceroy Nehru's "objection" to his scheme, for finding a solution, about which he had written to Mountbatten earlier.

Gandhi's deep disappointment at the turn of events was writ large in his letter to Sardar Patel. "I see that there is a wide and frequent divergence of views between us," he wrote to Sardar. "In the circumstances, is it desirable that I should see the Viceroy even in my individual capacity?"[26]

Gandhi's distress was no less visible in what he wrote to the Viceroy. "I had several short talks with Pandit Nehru, and had an hour's talk with him alone, and then with several members of the Congress Working Committee about the formula I had sketched before you and which I had filled in for them with all the implications ... I do not know that, having failed to carry both the head and heart of Pandit Nehru with me, I would have wanted to carry the matter further ... I felt sorry that I could not convince them of the correctness of my plan from every point of view. Nor could they dislodge me from my position although I had not closed my mind against every argument. Thus, I have to ask you to omit me from your consideration."[27]

The question was not put before the Congress Working Committee for a decision.

What was Nehru's "objection" to the scheme that Gandhi wanted to discuss with the Viceroy for a solution? Prof. Stanley Wolpert, Professor of

Indian History at the University of California at Los Angles and author of several books on India, explains in his book *Jinnah of Pakistan*.

"Gandhi's offer would never be conveyed to Jinnah," writes Prof. Wolpert. "Mountbatten opted first to discuss the matter with Nehru, whose reaction was totally negative. Nehru was shocked to learn that his Mahatma was quite ready to replace him as premier with Jinnah. After telling Mountbatten how 'unrealistic' Gandhi's solution was, Jawaharlal said, he was anxious for Gandhi to stay a few days longer in Delhi" as he had been away for several months and "was rapidly getting out of touch with events at the Centre."

Nehru and Patel "hoped quickly to bring the impractical old man back into 'touch' with their conclusions on how to handle Jinnah and the Muslim League." Prof. Wolpert delves deeper into the dilemma that India faced and the only solution that had the possibility of saving the Indian unity at that point of time. "There was a chance that the Mahatma's solution may have worked and saved the country," wrote Prof. Wolpert. "Perhaps even if Jinnah was offered the entire Central Government on a platter with the whole Cabinet under his personal control, he might have dismissed it with a negative wave of his long-fingered hand. Yet it was an exquisite temptation to place before him. It was a brilliant solution to India's oldest, toughest, greatest political problem. The Mahatma alone was capable of such absolute abnegation, such instant reversal of political position. Gandhi understood Jinnah well enough, moreover, to know just how potent an appeal to his ego that sort of singularly generous offer would have been. It might just have worked: surely this was a King Solomon solution. But Nehru had tested the cup of power too long to offer its necter to anyone else, least of all to Quaid-e-Azam (Jinnah)."

It is not without significance what Nehru had later told Ambassador Galbraith. "You realise Galbraith, I am the last Englishman to rule in India." Galbraith has recorded that Nehru made no secret of his British background and its influence on his political thought. Strange as it may appear, it extended to most things British—including the political solution that British rammed down India's throat, even against the wishes of Gandhi, who was not averse to the country ultimately getting divided, if it became necessary, by mutual discussion with the Muslim League, after the British had left India in whatever shape it wanted at the end of June 1948. But then it would have been an India solution.

Although all along vehemently opposed to dominion status under the British in earlier years, with himself in the seat of power, Nehru found no problem in accepting that status, sugar-coated as the offer was of getting full power soon in his hands even before British were to leave India. Strange again as it may appear, in this Nehru sadly got support from a very unexpected quarter: from the strongman of the Congress and one of the staunchest followers of Gandhi, Sardar Vallabhbhai Patel.

With Congress support it would have been very difficult for Jinnah "to refuse Mr. Gandhi's offer," Mountbatten had recorded, particularly in view of the frightening prospect of only "moth-eaten, truncated Pakistan" that was all that Jinnah was possibly to get, and which Jinnah had told the Viceroy would not be viable or economically workable. With Gandhi's backing the scheme the way he had volunteered to the Viceroy, and Jinnah's own assessment that "so far as the masses were concerned" Gandhi's was the "only name that would carry necessary weight"[28] from the Congress angle, it is difficult to think that Jinnah would not have played the game.

Thus it is as clear as daylight that the Congress leadership, headed by Nehru, failed to put its weight behind Gandhi's plan to give it even a fighting chance of succeeding to preserve the unity of India, even with some of their mental reservations. It was not that in the past often they had not persuaded themselves to follow the wisdom of Gandhi even when their own head sometimes had not supported them to do so. In the result they had invariably found vindication of Gandhi's wisdom as against their intellectual doubts. And at this point of time, it was the question of giving a last chance to the survival of India as a united entity.

At worst, Gandhi's plan may have failed to deliver the desired result. Partition of the country would then have followed with no worse consequences than what had taken place. There was, however, every chance that at least the country would have been spared the holocaust and unprecedented migration of population that followed partition the way it was brought about.

Once the British had left, the Indians would have settled matters among themselves and would have divided the country, if necessary. Have not the Czechs and Slovaks of the former Czechoslovakia agreed to separate without bitterness or bloodbath? And has not the same happened when the federating republics of the Soviet Union decided to go their separate ways amicably?

With its long tradition of tolerance and cultural heritage, Gandhi had no doubt India was capable of performing better once the British left Indian shores. The Congress leadership, however, failed to give India that glorious chance.

5

Congress Breaches Gandhi's Trust

"The light has gone out of our lives and there is darkness everywhere," mourned Nehru when Gandhi made his supreme sacrifice. "That light," he said, "represented the living truth ... reminding us of the right path, drawing us from error, taking this ancient country to freedom."[1]

Nehru and the Congress leaders had, however, refused to follow the "right path" even when Gandhi reminded them about it during the final hours of the test in the nation's history. Neither did they listen to him when he tried in deep anguish to "draw" them away from committing the grave "error" against this "ancient country."

What had led to this metamorphosis which made the undisputed general of the freedom struggle find in the last phase that his view no more counted with the Congress leadership—most of them built and brought up by him—in taking vital decisions about the future of the nation?

Gandhi had been the supreme master of the Congress for over three decades since he "for the first time entered the Congress" soon after the First World War "and immediately brought a complete change."[2] All the battles with the British Government had been fought by the Congress under Gandhi's leadership.

Between Gandhi and Nehru a "father-son relationship" had developed over the years, and the Mahatma had announced that it was "on Nehru's shoulder that he wished his mantle to fall."[3] This had, however, not prevented Gandhi from asking Nehru to resign from the Congress Working Committee for his reservations about launching of the "Quit India" movement in 1942, when Gandhi had simultaneously advised Maulana Azad to relinquish the Presidentship of the Congress for the doubts Azad shared with Nehru.

Mahadev Desai, Gandhi's Principal Secretary, has left a pen-picture of Gandhi's determined unconcern with regard to the course that Azad and Nehru might adopt in response to his directive. Both Nehru and Azad, however, had withdrawn their opposition to launching of the "Quit India" movement after a meeting with Gandhi when, according to Desai, "they understood the length" to which Gandhi was "prepared to go."[4]

A perceptible change in the Congress leaders' attitude had, however, taken place by the time they emerged from their long imprisonment in 1945 after the "Quit India" movement. "It was well known," Pyarelal had recorded, "that some of the tallest in the Congress had actually cried 'never again' during their last detention ... They were afraid again to go into wilderness ... Their last experience had in fact tinged their outlook and political philosophy ... Very few were really ready to adopt the way of blood, sweat and tears."[5]

The picture changed further with the formation of the interim government in 1946 when the top-ranking Congress leaders found themselves in the seat of power. They now had the state machinery at their disposal.

Jayaprakash Narayan, the leader of the Congress Socialists, had noted the change that was coming over the Congress leaders. "He wanted the Congress to use its enormous mass appeal to launch a countrywide agitation to prevent partition" noted a writer, but found that "the Congress was too eager to grasp power and too weary after years of struggle to launch another movement." He warned that if the Congress leadership persisted in "its attempt to transform the Congress into a mere parliamentary body ... relying entirely on governmental machinery to serve or rule over the people, turning more and more bureaucratic, keeping its hold over the Congress organisation by the distribution of patronage and largesse," the Congress Socialists would "unavoidably be drawn into conflict with it."[6]

"Nehru's devotion to Gandhi remained total," wrote the author of *Freedom at Midnight*, "but a subtle change was overtaking their relationship. A phase in Nehru's life was coming to a close."[7] The same was true with most of the Congress leadership. They would hereafter prefer to follow their own wisdom, rather than their heart or Gandhi.

And so when the fruit of the long freedom struggle loomed large over the horizon after the British announced their intention to quit India not later than June 1948, the Congress leaders had no hesitation in ignoring and bypassing the Mahatma, who had brought them to the threshold of freedom. Against Gandhi's repeated advice and warnings, they allowed themselves to become willing partners with the British in dividing their motherland. "The

Congress dropped the pilot," recorded Gandhi's secretary and biographer Pyarelal. Gandhi did not drop them.

The Congress leaders were no more willing to stand up and be counted in favour of a united India, and to face wilderness once again for the sake of the unity of the country, if necessary. The heroes of the freedom struggle had obviously developed cold feet; they were willing to go for an easy way out without taking into consideration the inherent consequences, against which Gandhi had warned them.

"The truth is that we were tired men and we were getting on in years too," Nehru confessed in 1956 to his biographer Michael Brecher. "Few of us could stand the prospect of going to prison again, and if we had stood out for a united India ... prison obviously awaited us. The plan for partition offered a way out and we took it."

The leaders had earlier begun to ignore the wellestablished norms and conventions followed by the Congress in the past. The Congress President, or whosoever was nominated by the Congress, had been representing the Congress in all its negotiations with the Government. In the early 1930s Gandhi had been nominated by the Congress as its sole representative to attend the Round Table Conference in London. In 1942, it was the Congress President who had conducted negotiations with Sir Stafford Cripps sent to India by the War Cabinet. In 1945 when the Viceroy Lord Wavell invited Gandhi "as the recognised leader" of the Congress to attend the Simla Conference to break the political deadlock, Gandhi had politely told the Viceroy that "in the forthcoming official conference, I can have no official position ... unless I become an official representative of the Congress." That function, Gandhi reminded Wavell, belonged to the Congress President "or whomsoever he and his Committee may appoint for the purpose."[8] It was again the Congress President who conducted negotiations, in 1946, with the British Cabinet Mission.

By the time the last Viceroy, Mountbatten, arrived in India in early 1947, Nehru, Patel, Azad, Rajendra Prasad and Rajagopalachari had all, however, joined the Interim Government as the Congress nominees and J. B. Kripalani had taken over as the Congress President. The leaders in the Government— Nehru and Patel in particular—did not consider it necessary to make it clear to Mountbatten that as far as the Congress was concerned the Viceroy had to deal and negotiate with the Congress President or whomsoever the Congress nominated for the purpose, and not with them as the Congress representatives in the Government. This was in marked contrast to the stand that Nehru had himself taken only a few months earlier. "Your invitation ... to confer with you ... about Interim Government placed me in somewhat difficult position," Nehru had written to Wavell in June 1946. "Our official spokesman in regard to such matters is naturally our President, Maulana Azad. He can speak and confer authoritatively, which I cannot do."[9]

Gandhi all along remained consistent and correct in his stand. When Mountbatten suggested an appeal for communal peace under the joint signatures of Gandhi and Jinnah, Gandhi had told the Viceroy that he would have no objection in signing the appeal provided Kripalani, who alone could represent the Congress, also signed as Jinnah was to sign the appeal in his capacity as the Muslim League President. Gandhi did not suggest Nehru's name on behalf of the Congress. On being informed by the Viceroy that Jinnah would agree to sign the appeal if the other signature was that of Gandhi alone, Gandhi telegraphed Mountbatten that he was "Of opinion President Congress should also sign. You should know reason for exclusion of the President of Congress."[10] Gandhi, however, left the final decision to Nehru, and the Viceroy had no difficulty in getting Nehru to leave the decision to him.

Mountbatten's wisdom by then had become more acceptable to Congress leaders than Gandhi's. Nehru had told the Viceroy that Gandhi "was rapidly getting out of touch with events at the Centre."[11] It is revealing to note what Mountbatten's biographer recorded about the emerging development at this point of time.

"In offering a glimpse into the growing gulf," separating Gandhi and his closest companions, wrote the biographer, Nehru's words provided the Viceroy with "a vital insight into the form his action ... should take. If he could not persuade Indian leaders to keep their country united he was going to have to persuade them to divide it. Gandhi's unremitting hostility to partition could place an insurmountable barrier in his path. His only hope in that event would be to persuade the leaders of the Congress to break with their leader and agree to divide India." Only Nehru, the Viceroy had come to the conclusion, "might have the authority to stand out against the Mahatma ... Mountbatten might be forced to widen and exploit that gap. He spared no effort to win Nehru's support."[12] The strategy worked with devastating effect.

When Gandhi presented to an "astonished" Viceroy the outline of his plan that Jinnah should be given the option to form the government, with the Congress supporting it, in order to prevent partition of the country by the British, Mountbatten had told Gandhi that his plan had "many attractions" for him. But no sooner did the Viceroy learn from Gandhi that Nehru had "at least one vital objection" to his plan, which Gandhi offered to discuss with the Viceroy to find a solution if Mountbatten considered his proposal workable, the Viceroy was persuaded by his advisers not to put his weight behind Gandhi's scheme.[13] "There was a nervous apprehension," recorded Gandhi's Secretary Pyarelal, "that Pandit Nehru might succumb to Mahatma's influence if he remained under the impression that the Viceroy favoured the Mahatma's plan."[14]

The Viceroy's advisers did not want Gandhi's plan to succeed, recorded Kripalani, the Congress President, "as it would upset their plan of partitioning India." Patel, they knew, was against it. "But they were afraid that Jawaharlal might fall in line" with Gandhi and under their "combined influence the Congress Working Committee might accept it. They knew by then the great influence that Mountbatten exercised over the judgement of Jawaharlal. They, therefore, conveyed to him that the Viceroy had not accepted the plan."[15] Consequently Nehru saw many difficulties in the plan and was therefore not in a position to support it.

Breaching the trust reposed in them by the nation and Gandhi, and without any mandate from the Congress, Nehru and Patel gave their consent to Mountbatten on behalf of the Congress for the partition. "This step was taken without any prior discussion in the Working Committee," recorded Kripalani. "This was the foretaste of things to come—not the organisation but the government it had put in power was the Congress."[16]

Gandhi was "the one potential grave danger" in executing his partition plan, Mountbatten had told Churchill. "But with the help of Nehru and Patel, he hoped he could contain him in a crisis."[17]

After they had already given their consent to Mountbatten for division on behalf of the Congress, Nehru wrote to him that the Congress President should also be invited to the conference where Mountbatten was to unfold his plan to the Indian leaders. "He represents the Congress formally and officially," wrote Nehru to Mountbatten, and that he himself and the other Congress leader Patel, in the government, who had been invited to attend "cannot be said to represent the Congress formally."[18] In the back ground in which the Congress leaders had carried out negotiations with him, the Viceroy neither considered it essential nor even necessary to concede Nehru's request. "I am afraid I do not feel able to accede to your suggestion … I confined all the talks since I have been out here with yourself (and) Sardar Patel," wrote back Mountbatten to Nehru.[19]

It was the Congress Working Committee, however, which forced Mountbatten to invite Kripalani to represent the Congress "formally and officially" at the conference. "The very first point that was raised" in the Working Committee, wrote Nehru to the Viceroy a fortnight later, was about "the invitations to your conference. Was the Congress represented in any way, I was asked, or were only the members of the Interim Government represented? ... I told them that I had written to you in the matter and gave them the purport of your reply. They were far from satisfied ... Both Sardar Patel and I would feel embarrassed if we have to go to this conference without Mr. Kripalani."[20]

Foreseeing the disaster that partition of the country meant, the statesman in Gandhi tried every means at his disposal to draw away the Congress leaders from the grave error they were bent upon committing. He wanted them to face the challenge squarely after the British had left India instead of caving in. The non-violent revolutionary in Gandhi was not afraid to face even a civil war after the British left. Gandhi had warned the Viceroy that it would be a "blunder of first magnitude" for the British to be party to partition and that "if it has to come, let it come as a result of understanding between the parties or an armed conflict." The Congress leaders, however, were not willing to face such a situation. They had taken precautions that Gandhi's wisdom did not prevail over their own decision.

"The disease of old age and exhaustion had come over this fighting organisation of freedom in its moment of greatest distress," recorded Dr. Lohia, a colleague of Nehru.[21] "The men were old and tired ... They had begun looking back on their life of struggle with a sense of hopeless despair. Their leader was not allowing them to temporise ... Some may have been hungering for the office and the power and comfort and pelf ... Some may have been wanting to change their country and leave their mark on history" by running the government "for some years at least before their death."[22]

Gandhi, who never sought anything for himself, alone, even at his age of three score and eighteen, was ready to face the biggest crisis in the history of the nation to preserve its unity and integrity, and was willing to wrestle with the gathering storm on the horizon.

6

Gandhi Considered Partition Preventable

In 1947 India was divided and the country became free. It was, however, not the kind of freedom for which generations of Indian people had fought and had willingly passed through fire, blood and tears.

In the euphoria of independence people had failed to comprehend that the Congress leadership were equally guilty for the partition of India along with Jinnah, the leader of the Muslim League. Gandhi, who had opposed the division till the last was, however, perceived by a group of misguided people as the person responsible for the division of India—the assassin Nathuram Godse being one of them.

Mountbatten had seen his predecessor Wavell returning to England dismissed and in disgrace for his failure to disentangle the Indian situation for the British. Distasteful though the possibility of the division of India might have been to him, for Mountbatten it was to be no greater tragedy than his not being able to return home in a blaze of glory. Preventing partition was therefore not his first priority. By the time he came to replace Wavell as the Viceroy, by a strange coincidence, it no more remained a priority with the Congress leaders either.

Announcing the appointment of Mountbatten as the Viceroy, Prime Minister Attlee had declared that "it was their definite intention ... to effect transference of power into responsible Indian hands by a date not later than June 1948." And only a few months earlier his three Cabinet colleagues had emphatically expressed their inability, at the end of prolonged negotiations with the Indian parties in the summer of 1946, "to advise the British Government that the power which at present resides in British hands should be handed over to two entirely separate sovereign states."[1]

The bitter experience of working with the Muslim League representatives in the Interim government had, however, completely changed the outlook of the Congress leaders by the time Mountbatten arrived in Delhi in March 1947. They had also by then built bridges with the bureaucracy, whose political advice they had begun to consider wise and acceptable. And the Congress leaders were in a hurry, unwilling to wait till the British left in less than fifteen months, to rule the country.

V. P. Menon, the Reforms Commissioner to the Viceroy, had recorded that in early 1947, within a few months of Congress leaders joining the government, Sardar Patel had signified to him his acceptance of Pakistan. Having thus made up his mind, one finds Patel sending signals to Jinnah through a common friend in the following words: "If the League insists on Pakistan, the only alternative is the division of Punjab and Bengal. They cannot have Punjab as a whole or Bengal."[2]

The long distance that the Congress leaders had travelled from their position in a very short period after joining the Government would be clear from the stand Patel had taken with the Viceroy only a year earlier. "He did not see how there was ever going to be a settlement between Hindus and Muslims while the British were in India," Wavell had recorded about his talk with Patel in January 1946, "and that the British should clear out and leave Indians to settle matters themselves."[3]

The Congress adopted the resolution demanding partition of the Punjab into Hindu and Muslim majority zones on the eve of Mountbatten's arrival without consulting Gandhi, and Nehru wrote to the Mahatma in reply to his letter that he felt convinced that indeed "this is the only answer to the partition as demanded by Jinnah."[4] Gandhi, of course, was not convinced.

To his relief, and somewhat to his surprise, Mountbatten thus found that instead of encountering any anticipated resistance to discussing probable partition of the country, the Congress leaders in the government—Nehru and Patel—had begun to support division of the country almost with the zeal of a convert. Within a fortnight of his arrival, the Viceroy was therefore recording that Jinnah was "determined to have Pakistan and Congress, with the exception of Mr. Gandhi, appeared to let him have it."[5]

Mountbatten had also recorded that he "regarded it a very great tragedy to give up the idea of a united India." He failed, however, to use the brilliant escape route that Gandhi provided him to prevent that "great tragedy." He also did not use his authority and undoubted persuasive power to advise the Congress leaders—Nehru, in particular—that they should put their weight behind Gandhi's scheme to give the unity of India a final chance of survival.

The classic example of his prevailing upon and persuading the Congress leaders was to make them agree to a referendum in the North-West Frontier Province, for or against becoming part of Pakistan, and not to support the demand of their comrades in that Province, which Gandhi considered right and just. In doing so, they hurt Gandhi deeply. "Would it be wrong," wrote Gandhi to Nehru, "if you insisted that referendum would be wrong without the presentation of the picture of Pakistan?" And he added: "The more I contemplate the difference in outlook and opinion between ... the Working Committee and me (the more) I feel that my presence (in Delhi) is unnecessary even if it is not detrimental to the cause we all have at heart."[6]

A wholly Muslim League Government headed by Jinnah at the Centre, supported by the Congress in the Assembly, to enable the British to leave India united, as envisaged in Gandhi's plan, might have made "Jinnah and his Muslim Leaguers less fanatical on the issue of partition and more receptive to the notion that the Congress Party and the Hindus wanted to play fair with them," wrote Ram Manohar Lohia, the Socialist leader, who used to be a special invitee to the Congress Working Committee meetings those days. "That such a scheme ... as might have kept India united, if it had succeeded, and would not have done the country the slightest harm, if it had failed, was given no serious consideration is proof that Congress leadership was concerned with matters of less than national import."[7]

The Congress leaders in the Government at least had their reason in not supporting Gandhi's scheme because "they were far too eager to do the business of governing by themselves."[8] The very idea of vacating the seat of power and authority that they had found after a long struggle, and handing it over to Jinnah was most distasteful to them.

Mountbatten, however, had nothing to lose if he backed Gandhi's scheme and persuaded the Congress leadership to do so to prevent what he himself had termed as a "very great tragedy."

The Viceroy might have failed in his efforts to make the Congress leaders agree to support Gandhi's scheme. But Mountbatten did not care even to try. Instead, on knowing from Gandhi that Nehru had certain objections to his plan, the Viceroy decided not to extend his support to the only plan that could have prevented division of the country.[9] Not unexpectedly, both Nehru and Patel told Gandhi that they could not support his plan.

The incorrigible optimist that Gandhi was, and the partition of the country by the British he considered such a disaster, that on finding his close colleagues had gone over into a different orbit, and realising that events were moving fast towards that great tragedy with the backing and support of the Congress leaders, Gandhi decided to make a final attempt to prevent partition through an appeal to the conscience of the British.

"Whatever may be said to the contrary," he told the Viceroy, "it would be a blunder of first magnitude for the British to be party in any way whatsoever to the division of India."[10] He advised the Viceroy "on no account to fall in the trap of making a decision on behalf of the British Government which would ultimately be regarded as a very wrong decision."[11] In making his anguished appeal to the British, Gandhi hoped that having taken in the past many a decision unilaterally against the interest of India, the British might, in that final hour, yet persuade themselves to do their last act right with India. If the division had to come, Gandhi had also told the Viceroy, "let it come after the (British) withdrawal, as a result of understanding between the parties or armed conflict."[12]

In a different age and clime, not very long ago, had not the Americans fought a bloody civil war—north against the south—for almost five years to prevent division of their country and to defend a principle? It made America what it had become, a great and powerful country.

Unlike his colleagues, who were determined to fight it out under their leader President Abraham Lincoln less than a hundred years earlier, the Indian leaders failed to comprehend the consequences of their decision to divide the country on communal lines and showed their unwillingness to follow their leader even when Gandhi placed before them a way to meet the most serious crisis in the history of India. Given a chance the Indian situation could not have been any different to what had happened in America, baptised by the fire of even a civil war, if necessary.

The Congress leadership, however, were scared at the very prospect of the trouble they might have to face after the British had gone and had no hesitation in throwing out of the window Gandhi's sound advice to stand firm against the partition. Sardar Patel, the Congress strongman, had no qualms even about letting the Viceroy know that "not too much account should be taken of the recent utterances of Mr. Gandhi in favour of a united India."[13] Mountbatten could well afford in that situation to ignore Gandhi's words of sanity, heed the tumult of "the chief priests" and the advice of the officials to proceed with the swift surgical operation.

The result of the unwillingness to follow Gandhi when the country faced the final call is now history: Even after fighting several wars, beginning with the first soon after partition of the country and the last only a few years ago, the two countries have not been able to settle down in peace with each other after sixty years of that great tragedy.

Having, however, already got Nehru and Patel firmly on his side, the Viceroy had no intention of abandoning his scheme to divide the country, or to act on Gandhi's advice. "Gandhi came to see me," the Viceroy cabled London reporting his talk with him. "I explained to him in broad outline the plan which Ismay had taken home. His comment was that it was quite wrong of the British to take any steps to facilitate the partition of India and he returned again to his original plan to demit power either to the League or to the Congress to run India as a whole."[14]

The British, however, had no intention of handing over a united India either to the Congress or to the Muslim League, to decide themselves after the British had gone, if they wished to remain united or would divide their motherland. The British would have left India by June 1948 in any case even if the Congress leaders had not agreed to the division of the country.

The Congress leaders were, however, not willing to wait till the British had gone, as Gandhi wanted them to do, instead of negotiating partition with the British. "Jawaharlal Nehru, who had been a strident advocate of complete independence as against dominion status," a political commentator recorded, "now agreed to partition and dominion status as the price of wielding power in diminished India. Gandhi acquiesced in partition out of his affection for Nehru, Patel and other lieutenants who had followed him for so long but were now tired—he himself was not, though much older than they."[15]

By giving their consent to partition against Gandhi's advice, Nehru, Patel and other Congress leaders were thus able to become masters of what had been left of a divided India a few months earlier than the date by which the British were to leave. And Gandhi, the soul and the liberator of the nation, was left to mourn the death of his dream of a lifetime, and to nurse a mortally wounded and bleeding India, receiving not much later, on January 30, 1948, three bullets on his chest fired from a pistol by Godse.

Gandhi had repeatedly declared "partition on my dead body," observed L. C. Jain. "So when Partition did happen before his eyes and he could not prevent it, he lost no time in handing his dead body to us and was dead in less than six months."

Though Mountbatten had the dubious distinction of dividing this great land of composite culture and heritage, he achieved glory for having accomplished the task of performing a quick surgical operation with the consent of the Indian parties. One does not, however, have to go far to find the hollowness of his achievement. "There is a big volume of opinion all over the world," a note that the Viceroy's office itself had sent to London at that time recorded, "that ways and means should have been found to keep India united and grave doubts have been expressed about the necessity of partition ... Gandhi in particular has often said that the British should quit and leave Indians to work out their own salvation."[16]

Who among the Congress leaders played the decisive role in allowing the British to divide the country? It is a difficult question to answer. Nehru was undoubtedly influenced most by the charm of the Mountbattens. The Viceroy has recorded that he had carried on all the negotiations with Pandit Nehru and Sardar Patel, mostly and primarily with Nehru, to the exclusion of all other Congress leaders. It is on record too that Gandhi had failed to get Nehru to support his scheme which could have averted partition. Between the two, Nehru obviously played the leading role and "step by step" allowed himself and the Congress to commit to the division of the country. In this he had no doubt the support of Patel.

There may have been many differences between Nehru and Patel—as indeed, there were—about timings and approach to various issues. Patel, the practical man that he was, may have handled the situation differently. Nehru's was an idealistic approach, Pyarelal has recorded. It lacked the sanction which Gandhi's leadership provided. "Sardar Patel, the ... realist, was at times very critical of ... the disjointed idealism of his colleague. But however much they disagreed with each other, neither of them could agree with Gandhiji" to prevent the division of India by the British.

Why had Gandhi surrendered on the issue of partition? Not an easy question. Pyarelal in his book *The Last Phase* has recorded Gandhi's answer. "The decision about Pakistan is of course wrong," Gandhi wrote to a colleague. "But against whom am I to fight and to what end?" Pyarelal has explained that Gandhi "could not resort to non-cooperation with his colleagues because their judgement differed from his own" about partition or "threaten his colleagues with sabotage ... because they felt unable to go his way... They continued to be his best friends though for the time he had lost his hold on them."

Gandhi was not a dictator. He never forced his views down the throat of his colleagues and followers. "On numerous occasions ... and on one ...

occasion, which determined the fate of India," Louis Fischer has recorded in his book, "Gandhi gave Congress a free hand even when he disliked the intended act of Congress. That was his nonviolence. Non-violence was more than ... non-hurting. It was freedom. Had he coerced his followers, he would have been a violent dictator."

Gandhi had influence. More than influence he had authority. But he eschewed power. "Power is the attribute of a machine; authority is the attribute of a person ... Gandhi's rejection of power enhanced his authority. Power feeds on the blood and tears of its victims. Authority is fed by service, sympathy and affection."[17]

The terrible price that the Indian subcontinent had to pay for not heeding Gandhi's advice—the Congress leadership, Jinnah, Mountbatten and the British Government, all of them guilty in equal measure—is well known and available in stark statistics: six hundred thousand women, children and men killed; fifteen million uprooted from their homes to become refugees in the biggest ever migration in human history. And opening of the floodgates of continuous and continuing conflict between the two parts of the divided subcontinent.

The creation of Pakistan had not solved the communal problem, Maulana Azad, one of the Congress leaders lived to record. "The basis of partition was enmity between Hindus and Muslims ... The subcontinent of India divided into two states looked at one another with hatred and fear. If we had remained steadfast and refused to accept Partition, I am confident that a safer and more glorious future would have awaited us."[18]

Partition produced that "which it was designed to avoid in such abundance," lamented Ram Manohar Lohia, "that one may for ever despair of man's intelligence or integrity."[19]

And Nehru was wiser after the event, when he confessed before an audience in New York two years later that he would have resisted division of India if he had known the terrible consequences of partition.

The long-term damage to the fragile secular fabric of India that partition has continued to do even after several decades of the event is not unknown. The dance of death and destruction that followed the demolition of the Babri mosque in Ayodhya at the end of 1992 and the carnival of death in Bombay and Surat that followed soon after in early 1993 are only its recent manifestations.

Writing under the heading "Death of a Concept," Zafar H. Jung recorded that "India and Pakistan as one entity representing two great religions—

Hinduism and Islam—would have withstood the challenges of the modern world better" but for the "devastation caused by the two-nation theory." He went on to add that "the myopic Muslim League became a willing tool in the hands of colonial master and succeeded ultimately in destroying the essence of Indianhood by splitting the country into two." Jung concluded that if the birth of Bangladesh subsequently had proved the futility of the two-nation theory, Pakistan's inability to integrate migrants from India with mainstream is not only the demise of the very "concept of Pakistan" but also gives the two-nation theory "the burial it ought to have got in 1947."[20]

It is one of the ironies of history, too deep even for tears, that while the Congress leaders were unable to comprehend the consequences of partition, they had no hesitation in ignoring Gandhi, who had brought them to the threshold of freedom, and clearly foreseeing the consequences, warned them against allowing the British to divide the country.

7

British Infamy Led to Partition

India won freedom from British rule in August 1947. In less than six months of this historic event, in January 1948, the nation lost its brightest star and the biggest asset—Mahatma Gandhi. The assassination of Gandhi, which left the people stunned all over the world, was the direct consequence of partition, forced on India by the British.

The Bible records that when Governor Pilate saw nothing would prevail with the crowd, who were misled by the "chief priests and the elders" to have Jesus crucified, "he took water, and washed his hands," saying, "I am innocent of the blood of this just person. It is your responsibility." The British did the same two thousand years later in dealing with India.

After ramming down the Indian throat the decision to divide the country, resulting in six hundred thousand women, men and children butchered and fifteen million people uprooted to become homeless refugees—the poison and hatred generated resulting in the assassination of Gandhi—the British washed their hands of all responsibility for the tragedy that India had to face. They had to divide the country, the British proclaimed to the world, because the "chief priests and the elders" of the Indian parties asked them to do so.

The world was, however, aware that above the din of the "chief priests," Gandhi had sounded the bell. He had advised the British to follow the path of sanity and justice towards the Indian nation when there was insanity all around. He had pleaded with them not to shatter the beautiful mosaic of composite culture and heritage of the subcontinent. In no uncertain terms Gandhi had sent them the message "on no account to fall in the trap of making a decision ... which will ultimately be regarded as a very wrong decision."[1] Instead of listening to these words of reason and wisdom, the British went ahead and cut the country into two.

The run-up of the last days of the British rule in India reads no different from the fable of the monkey dispensing justice between two cats except for the deep human tragedy as its essential ingredient. It was a perfect no-win situation that the British forced on India. Of all the solutions that could emerge to meet the situation, the only acceptable one to the British was to divide the country before quitting India.

Only a year earlier the British Cabinet Mission had rejected the demand for the division of India. Within a few months, the British also announced their intention to quit India not later than the middle of 1948. Every step that the British took between the two announcements was, however, a downhill slide that forced the division of the country on the Indian people.

Jinnah, the Muslim League leader, had accepted the Cabinet Mission's recommendation for a loose Indian federation instead of pressing for his demand for the division of the country. He had then expressed his willingness to form an Interim government by himself; the Congress having declined to join as it had been denied the right to nominate any nationalist Muslim in the Government. The British, however, declined to accept Jinnah's offer because they wanted formation of a coalition government of both the Congress and the Muslim League to take over power from the British.

"The reactions of the Muslim League to my refusal to form an Interim government immediately were very hostile," wrote the Viceroy to Colville, the Governor of Bombay. "I think Jinnah and his Working Committee ... were bitterly disappointed at the cup being dashed from their lips. The terms ... would of course have been particularly attractive to Jinnah if the Congress had stayed out, and it may be that Jinnah's publication of his letter about the Nationalist Muslim issue ... was a deliberate attempt to keep the Congress out."[2]

Wavell was, however, left with no choice subsequently but to invite Nehru, the then Congress President, to form the Interim government by himself, as Jinnah had with drawn his cooperation by the time the Viceroy began a fresh attempt for the formation of a coalition government. But Wavell felt deeply unhappy and uneasy with the Congress alone in the government. He spared no effort to bring in the Muslim League in whatever way possible and had his way to persuade the League to join the government without even any basic understanding between the two parties about the functioning of the coalition government.

There could have been no stranger way to form a coalition interim government which was to take over power from the British than the way the

League accepted the Viceroy's invitation to do so. The Muslim League did not approve "of the basis and scheme of setting up the Interim Government," wrote Jinnah to Wavell, "and cannot agree with your decision already taken, nor with the arrangements you have already made." The Muslim League had, however, for "various reasons come to the conclusion that in the interests of Mussalmans ... it will be fatal to leave the entire field of administration of the Central Government in the hands of the Congress" and would therefore join the Government on the Viceroy's invitation.[3]

"It is obvious that the League wish to come in," Wavell himself had recorded, "and that the coalition government, if formed, will not be all pulling in the same direction."[4] But this is precisely what the Viceroy succeeded in achieving.

"You are a great soldier—a daring soldier," Gandhi had written to the Viceroy when Wavell failed in his earlier attempt to constitute a coalition of both the parties. "Dare to do the right. You must make your choice of one horse or the other. So far as I can see you will never succeed in riding two at the same time ... For God's sake do not make an incompatible mixture and in trying to do so produce a fearful explosion."[5]

Wavell's experiment with the formation of a coalition government, which was divided against itself, finally produced the "fearful explosion" in the shape of a sharp deterioration in the law and order situation all over the country. It also truly laid the foundation for the partition of the country. The experience of the Muslim League Ministers refusing to allow the government to function as a team led the Congress leaders to abandon their age-old ideal of keeping India united. And so Mountbatten found on his arrival in Delhi in March 1947 that while Jinnah was determined to have Pakistan, the Congress, except Gandhi, had no objection to dividing the country.[6]

Like the real mother in the story of Solomon's judgement, Gandhi advised the Congress leaders to come out of the Government and give over the country to Jinnah to rule, and to extend to him support in the Assembly, instead of becoming a party with the British to the division of their motherland. Gandhi was certain that Jinnah would become "less fanatical on the issue of partition and more receptive to keeping India united" by his experience that the Congress "wanted to play fair with them."[7]

Mountbatten had recorded that he "regarded it as a very great tragedy to give up the idea of a united India."[8] He had expressed that Gandhi's plan had, therefore, "many attractions" for him.[9] He had noted that "Gandhi's amazing personal influence ... might induce the Congress to accept" his plan. "He had learnt from Maulana Azad and Abdul Ghaffar Khan, the two Congress leaders, that Gandhi's plan was perfectly feasible of being carried out."[10]

Yet Mountbatten did precious little to retain the unity of India by adopting that plan even after knowing that "it would not be very easy for Mr. Jinnah to refuse Mr. Gandhi's offer."[11]

On the contrary, no sooner Mountbatten learnt from Gandhi that Nehru had some objection to Gandhi's plan, he lost no time to let him know that he was not in any way committed to Gandhi Plan,[12] instead of persuading Nehru to put his weight behind that plan or to give opportunity to Gandhi to sort out Nehru's objection by indicating his own support to the only plan that could have averted partition.

"If we had not been credulous," recorded Kripalani, the Congress President, "we could have known that Mountbatten was only carrying out the designs and will of the white bureaucracy here. They had carefully and cleverly set the stage for the partition of the country. Mountbatten might toy with the idea of a united India or, as Gandhi had suggested, with the plan of handing over India to Jinnah and League. But ... he found the division plan ... more convenient."[13]

Visualising the terrible consequences that would follow if the British insisted on dividing the country in the surcharged atmosphere with bitterness and hatred at the boiling point, Gandhi tried to put reason into his own people as well as in the hearts of the British. "We are unable to think coherently whilst British power is still functioning in India," Gandhi exhorted for all those who would listen. "Its function is not to change the map of India ... Today, in the presence of the British power, we are only demoralised ... After it is withdrawn ... we shall have the wisdom to think coherently and keep India one or split it into two parts or more."[14] Gandhi was not afraid even to face a civil war after the British withdrawal and had told the Viceroy that it would be a blunder for the British to be party in any way to the division of India.[15]

"Did Mountbatten rush India ... into partition without foreseeing the disastrous consequences? Or was he warned of the likely results and simply ignored all advice?" asks Brian Hoey in his book *Mountbatten—The Private Story*. He answers his question by recording that "there is little doubt that from time to time" Mountbatten's "ambition clouded his judgment."

History's verdict to what a mess Mountbatten had left did not take long to come. "Nothing in the twentieth century was so badly handled and with such disastrous consequences," wrote Prof. Galbraith, the distinguished economist of Harvard University, who had worked with and for half a dozen Presidents of the USA from Roosevelt to Kennedy and had also been US Ambassador to India, "as Mountbattten's policies on Indian Independence, leading as they did to the division of the subcontinent into three countries amidst conflict, mass magration and death."

"It was bad enough that the vain, self-serving and utterly unqualified Lord Mountbatten was sent out to manage the final stages of independence," commented Paul Mann in *New York Times*, reviewing the book *India's Long Road to Independence*. "The whole process was fraught with an almost unbelievable banality ... A partition executed with such heinous incompetence that it resulted in the deaths of one million people and caused millions of others to be driven forcibly from their homes."

Paul Mann concludes his review by saying that "to comprehend the damage this must have done to the national psyches of both the countries, just consider for a moment, if here in America, the Confederacy had stayed separate and North and South were now nuclear armed and at each other's throats over unresolved issues ... like the division of California ... What the book reveals is just how comprehensively India and Pakistan were betrayed ... by the British."

The British plan, Mountbatten had tried to soothe Gandhi, gave Indians freedom of choice: to divide the country or to keep it united. Gandhi pointed out to the Viceroy in reply that he should remain under no such delusion; what the British were planning to do was just the opposite. They were not "leaving the people of India a free choice" since they were "practically imposing partition on them."[16]

No less a person than the Secretary of State for India had confirmed what Gandhi told the Viceroy. "I do not suggest that he (Mountbatten) should act as arbitrator in disputes," Lord Listwell wrote to Prime Minister Attlee within a fortnight of the announcement of the partition plan. "But there may be occasions on which the Indians, while unable to agree, will accept something virtually imposed by him, as they have done in effect over partition."[17]

There were few takers even among the enlightened Englishmen for the sham argument that Indians were given a free choice. "I do not accept the statement," one of them stated in the British Parliament, "that the people (of India) were responsible for the partition any more than the people of Ireland were responsible for the partition of Ireland."[18]

Gandhi's pleadings had thus not produced any different effect on the British than the message sent by his wife had on Pilate at the trial of the Prince of Peace two thousand years earlier. "Have thou nothing to do with that just man," Pilate's wife had said in her message. Brushing aside this advice, the Governor fell in line with the clamour of the "chief priests," washed his hands and condemned Jesus to be crucified. Gandhi's words of reason and wisdom were similarly brushed aside by the British and they went ahead to cut the country into two as if it were a piece of cake.

* * *

Did Mountbatten in later years feel any different about the way he handled the situations resulting in the great tragedy of the partition? We find some inkling about it from what the distinguished Professor of Indian History at the University of California in Los Angeles has recorded in his book *Shameful Flight: The Last Years of the British Empire in India* published in 2006.

"The tragedy of partition and its more than half a century legacy of hatred, fear and continued conflict ... might well have been avoided," noted Stanley Wolpert in his book, "or at least mitigated but for the arrogance and ignorance of a handful of British and Indian leaders ... Those ten additional months of talks aborted by an impatient Mountbatten, might have helped all parties to agree that cooperation was much wiser than conflict, dialogue more sensible than division."

After expressing his views, the distinguished historian tells us about a meeting that John Osman of BBC had with Mountbatten eighteen years after Partition and shortly after Indian-Pakistan war of 1965. When asked how he felt about his Indian Viceroyalty, Mountbatten admitted to John Osman, when they sat next to one another at a dinner, that he had "got things wrong." Osman felt "sympathy" for the remorseful sixty-five-years-old ex-Viceroy and tried to cheer him up," but to no avail.

Another thirty-five years after that meeting, in an article in *The Spectator* in September 2004, Osman recalled that Mountbatten was not to be consoled. "To this day his own judgment on how he had performed in India rings in my ears and in my memory. As one who dislikes the tasteless use in writing ... 'vulgar slang'! ... shall permit myself an exception this time because it is the only honest way of reporting accurately what the last Viceroy of India thought the way he had done his job: 'I fucked it up."

In another article in *The Independent*, under the heading "British Revisits Partition on 60th Anniversary," Adrian Hamilton recorded the British

Perspective about Partition in the following words: "Indian partition had huge consequences, still very much with us today. But the manner and matter of it was primarily a British responsibility, of historical consequences to us more than the subjects of it ... The documentation as it has come out ... points a rather less flattering view of the dissolution of Empire ... In India at least the sordid truth is that we and in particular our last Viceroy Lord Mountbatten—cut and ran ... It is also true that Mountbatten rushed into partition ten months before the original date with barely a thought and certainly no properly prepared handover plan, for the consequences of his plan, for the consequences of his action. Vain, duplicitous ... and obsessed with his own reputation, the new Governor General came, saw and determined to get out before he could be blamed for what was bound to ensue ... . We should have set a reasonable deadline for British withdrawal and then worked out an agreed plan for security and civil authority to take us to it. We cut and ran 60 years ago."

* * *

There was nothing to celebrate the way independence was to be heralded with division of the country. His place, Gandhi was clear, was to be by the side of the minorities on both sides of the great divide, who were scared to death about their future in the land of their birth.

Pyarelal has given us a scintillating pen-picture of what was passing through Gandhi's mind. During his stay in Delhi in June and July of 1947, "a tumult raged within" Gandhi, Pyarelal tells us. If after achieving independence, Gandhi felt, the bottled-up passions burst forth "as it threatened to do," writes Pyarelal, he could do nothing to prevent such an eventuality. "He must be by the side of the people ... whose protection at the time of peril he had pledged his life." His place in the circumstance "was not in the capital but with the men of the tattered battalion, which fights till it dies." Pyarelal summed up Gandhi's thinking in the following verse:

"Theirs be the music, the colour, the glory, the gold;
Mine be a handful of ashes, a mouthful of mould.
Of the maimed, of the halt and the blind in the rain and the cold—
Of these shall my songs be fashioned, my tales be told."

Leaving behind the music, the colour and the glory for the leaders, Gandhi arrived in Calcutta on his way to Noakhali to keep his promise to be with the Hindu minority community there, which was scared to death at the prospect of becoming part of Pakistan, having suffered untold misery only some months ago under the Muslim League Government presided over by Suhrawardy in the aftermath of Great Calcutta Killings.

A number of Muslim leaders and delegations met Gandhi at Sodepur Ashram on his arrival there, followed by Suhrawardy himself, who was to lose his chair soon, to persuade Gandhi not to proceed to Noakhali but to stay back in Calcutta to prevent the blighted city from facing another round of carnage and killings, which according to them, was sure to happen as Hindus of the city were getting ready to avenge what had happened to them only a year earlier.

Gandhi found himself facing a dilemma: should he proceed to Noakhali to keep his promise to the frightened Hindu minority community there or should he stay back in Calcutta to prevent the Muslim minority form coming to harm from the Hindu majority of the city? It did not take him long to come to a decision. Gandhi came to the conclusion that his duty demanded that he should first remove the fear from the minds of Muslims of Calcutta, where the danger seemed real and imminent, and the dam of violence was likely to burst any time, before proceeding to Noakhali, provided certain conditions were fulfilled.

The conditions he spelt out were: one, the Muslim leaders of Calcutta should collectively guarantee peace in Noakhali; two, Suhrawardy would work with him for the restoration of peace in Calcutta; and three, both he and Suhrawardy would live under the same roof in one of the disturbed areas of the city, unprotected by police or military.

If Suhrawardy and other Muslim leaders accepted these conditions, he would postpone his going to Noakhali indefinitely and would remain in Calcutta as long as it was necessary. Gandhi advised Suhrawardy to consult his aged father and his only daughter before giving his consent, as the risk was great.

On receiving consent form Suhrawardy on his own behalf and on behalf of Muslim leaders, Gandhi announced his decision in his evening prayer meeting. He told the audience that he had been warned that Suhrawardy was not to be relied upon. But had not the same been told about him too? He would trust Suhrawardy as he expected to be trusted. He asked the gathering to bless the mission.

The change that this decision of Gandhi brought about in Calcutta would have been unimaginable even a few days earlier; it was nothing short of a miracle performed. No sooner had Gandhi moved to a Muslim house in Calcutta, to live there along with Suhrawardy, news began to reach him by the evening of the next day that a strange thing had started in different parts of Calcutta. "For one whole year Hindus and Muslims had avoided one another's company. Calcutta had virtually become divided into exclusively Hindu and Muslim zones. But news now began to pour in that Hindus and Muslims were both coming out in the streets and embracing one another." I had been an eyewitness to the unfolding events as I was spending all the time of each day under the same roof with the Mahatma and Suhrawardy. My impression of those days may appear exaggerated or the statement of an immature young man—I was only 21 years of age. I better therefore quote from what Prof. Dennis Dalton, the distinguished Head of the Department of Political Science of Barnard College of Columbia University, New York, has written about the events that followed Gandhi's decision to move into the disturbed area of Calcutta to stay unprotected by the police or military. However, before Dennis Dalton tells us about the unfolding events of that city, I would like to mention about the effect that the changed situation and atmosphere of Calcutta had on my young mind. Had I known the lines then, I would have surely sung with the Poet,

> Bliss was it in that dawn to be alive,
> But to be young was very heaven!

"Picture the scene of virtual civil war in Calcutta, with its large Muslim minority; unprecedented street violence began in August, 1946 with Great Calcutta Killings of over 4,000 Hindus and Muslim in 48 hours, and then continued unabated until the following August when India and Pakistan achieved independence," Dennis Dalton tells us.

Dennis Dalton puts on record "that fear and fury swept through the streets of Calcutta in the terrible year of communal massacres as the city, divided into two armed camps, came together only to inflict more daily violence on one another. The Calcutta *Statesman* recorded the grim statistics of the daily casualties, making it clear that neither police nor military could contain the slaughter. Into this cauldron stepped Gandhi in mid-August with one purpose, to bring peace to Calcutta."

"He first moved into the home of a Muslim friend," records Dennis. "When his example did not stop the killing, he began a fast for communal harmony, announcing that the fast would end when peace returned to the city. At first, in the initial 24 hours of the fast, the violence continued, but then as his condition worsened ... the people of Calcutta responded. Students, business groups ... trade unions, members of the press, all began to bring down the barricades and call for Hindu-Muslim unity. Gandhi broke his fast not just when the killings stopped, but only after representatives of all communities assured him that the violence would not return."

Dennis Dalton ends his note quoting E. W. R. Lumby, the closest historian of partition, as the verdict of history. "His triumph was complete," Lumby wrote, and the peace that he brought was destined to endure ... He had in fact worked a miracle, perhaps the greatest of modern times."

"In the Punjab we have 55,000 soldiers and large-scale rioting on our hands; in Bengal our forces consist of one man, and there is no rioting," Mountbatten, the GovernorGeneral, wrote to Gandhi referring to the peace he had ensued in the two parts of divided Bengal contrary to all forecasts. "As a serving officer, as well as an administrator I may be allowed to pay my tribute to the One Man Boundary Force."[19]

Mountabatten had, however, not been able to size up Gandhi even after five months of close contacts, meetings and exchange of correspondence. Below the surface of civility that he personified, Mountbatten continued to be cynical about all that Gandhi was doing and saying.

Gandhi "is now off to Noakhali," Mountbatten as the Viceroy had earlier reported to the British Government. "I can only hope that his presence there will not result in disturbance. But of this Burrows (Governor of Bengal) is not too sure."

If there could, however, be a prize for "double-speak," the message that Mountabatten had sent at the same time to London would surely deserve the cake: "Gandhi's absence from the celebrations in Delhi on the 15th August is, of course, intentional. He has never given the 3rd June plan (of partition) his unqualified blessing and his position may be difficult ... Gandhi has announced his decision to spend the rest of his life in Pakistan looking after the minorities. This will infuriate Jinnah, but will be a great relief to Congress for, as I have said before, his influence is largely negative or even destructive ... ."[20]

On the eve of his departure for Delhi, Calcutta witnessed a massive farewell meeting to be addressed by Gandhi. The crowd had been estimated to be around half a million strong, overflowing the big Calcutta Maidan. The meeting also witnessed the volunteers of the Congress and the Muslim League jointly supervising and regulating the unprecedented crowd that had gathered to hear Gandhi's speech to citizens of Calcutta. The present author was an eyewitness of the event surveying the amazing scene and massive gathering from the rostrum occupied by around a dozen leaders of both communities besides Gandhi.

By breaking his fast only after one day's absence of strife on the strength of the assurances of friends from all communities in Calcutta and outside, said Gandhi in his address to the gathering, he threw the burden on them for preservation of peace at the cost of their lives. Let them therefore not be guilty of having brought about his death. If unfortunately the peace was broken once again, there would be no alternative for him but to undertake a fast unto death. He could not, like a child play with them and each time say, he was going to break his fast if they resumed sanity. He had made that solemn declaration for Bihar, then for Noakhali and now for Calcutta. If God willed that he should still do some service, he would bless all with wisdom to do the right thing. Consider the consequence of Calcutta remaining sane. It must mean automatic sanity of all Bengal, East and West. It meant also Bihar and consequently the Punjab, where God was sending him. And if the Punjab came to its senses the rest of India was bound to follow.

From Calcutta Gandhi rushed to prop "the crumbling heavens" in the two parts of the Punjab. On his way he found that Delhi too was aflame. He soon brought Delhi back to sanity. But the demon released by the great tragedy of partition was lurking not far behind him all along. It finally got the opportunity to claim Gandhi's life on January 30, 1948, in less than six months of India achieving its independence.

⁂

8

Gandhi and the Congress

"And then Gandhi came," Nehru had recorded about the Mahatma's coming into the Congress at the end of the First World War. "He was like a powerful current of fresh air that made us stretch ourselves and take deep breaths; like a beam of light that pierced the darkness and removed the scales from our eyes."[1]

Gandhi "immediately brought about a complete change" in the Congress. From an annual show he converted it "into an efficient, well-knit and highly disciplined instrument of action."[2] Over the years, thereafter, the Congress leaders followed Gandhi's wisdom even when often their head did not support their doing so. They invariably found vindication of Gandhi's wisdom as against their own intellectual doubts. Nehru had opposed almost all of Gandhi's great moves against the British initially, wrote the author of *Freedom at Midnight*. "But his heart had told him to follow the Mahatma and his heart, he would later admit, had been right."[3]

Three decades later when Gandhi made the supreme sacrifice at the altar of the demon released by partition of the country, Nehru expressed his anguish to the world in the following words: "The light has gone out of our lives ... the living truth represented ... reminding us of the right path, drawing us from error, taking this ancient country to freedom."[4]

What then had led the Congress leaders to defy Gandhi and not to follow the "right path" shown by him when he had tried to draw them away from committing the "error" of unprecedented dimension in the final testing hours in the history of this "ancient country" to allow the British to divide the country in the teeth of Gandhi's opposition? And what was the reason for them not to heed his advice, after independence, to disband the Congress in its existing form and to dedicate itself to the attainment of social, moral and economic freedom of the masses?

The last phase of the freedom struggle, recorded Pyarelal, "marked the beginning of that cleavage" between Gandhi and some of his closest Congress colleagues "which in the final phase of transfer of power left them facing different ways."[5] Gandhi's insistence "on being left alone to settle directly with the Muslim League after the British had quitted, even if it meant civil war, rather than enter into ... a deal with the British" and his advice to allow the British to hand over power to Jinnah instead of negotiating partition with them, had left the Congress leaders out of their breath "with their purely political approach."[6]

The different settings in which the old guards had been functioning since joining the Government a few months before independence had conditioned their thinking, outlook and approach differently. The leaders had by then also been drawn into a different orbit—the orbit of the new Viceroy. "Lord Mountbatten found in Congress leaders apt pupils," wrote Pyarelal. Not Gandhi but "they were the ones, the word went round, with whom business could be done."[7]

Mountbatten had realised early that if he could not get the Muslim League to agree to keep India united, he would have to make the Congress leaders to agree to its division. But Gandhi's uncompromising opposition to any partition by the British would make it very difficult, if not impossible, for him to persuade the Congress leaders to break with Gandhi. And among the Congress leaders Nehru alone, the Viceroy had come to the conclusion, "might have the authority to stand out against the Mahatma."[8] Mountbatten, therefore, spared no effort to win over Nehru.

"I think you realise my difficulties with Nehru; they are partly political and partly psychological," Mountbatten had pleaded with the Punjab Governor Jenkins, who had complained that Nehru was "wrong in his facts and reasoning" in accusing British officers of partiality. While assuring the Governor that he considered Nehru's allegations "completely absured," the Viceroy told him that he was in no position to take up the matter with Nehru as "Nehru's goodwill is essential to me in this critical transition period."[9]

The Viceroy used "Krishna Menon as contact with Nehru and V. P. Menon as contact with Patel."[10] Mountbatten had great confidence in the ability of his Reforms Commissioner V. P. Menon, and he had found Krishna Menon to be Nehru's "greatest friend"[11] whose "complete confidence he has."[12] The Viceroy recorded that through Krishna Menon "I have been able to be particularly well informed about the Congress thought and opinion ... (and) with V. P. Menon and his close contact with Vallabhbhai Patel I have been able to know all that has been going on in both camps in the Congress Party."[13]

"The fact that the more sane elements of the Congress, and especially Vallabhbhai Patel, were at this stage prepared to do business," recorded Mountbatten's secretary Abell, "enabled the Viceroy to use V. P. (Menon) and his influence with Patel to a remarkable effect. The second point, of course, was that the moment the Muslim League definitely realised what was the maximum they could get out of HMG they began for the first time to be sensible."[14]

In this scenario the Viceroy needed the goodwill and support of neither Gandhi nor of the Congress President. Mountbatten had also found that Nehru and Patel had no objection to Gandhi being "put on pedestal, admired ... consulted, listened to with respectful attention and bypassed."[15]

The Viceroy had, thus, no difficulty in getting Nehru and Patel to commit themselves, "step by step"—Nehru's words—without "consulting their colleagues, including the Congress President" and of course Gandhi.[16] The Viceroy could, in the situation, well afford even to turn down Nehru's request to associate the Congress President—"he represents the Congress formally and officially. Others may be prominent Congressmen, but they ... cannot be said to represent Congress formally"—with the final talk about the partition plan[17] because Mountbatten had all his talks "since I have been out here with yourself (and) Sardar Patel."[18]

Gandhi was opposed to the very logic of partition by the British. For him to ask for partition was a counsel of despair. He had, therefore, striven with the Congress leaders for the acceptance of the plan that he had outlined to the Viceroy to prevent such a calamity. He had no doubt that "partition would solve none of their difficulties. On the contrary, it would accentuate those that were already there and create fresh ones."

On finding that Nehru and Patel between them had irrevocably committed the Congress to break the unity of the country, Gandhi advised them that even this decision on their part need not necessarily come in the way of allowing any affected Province, where both the communities so desired, to remain united and even independent of India and Pakistan, instead of being divided for one part to become part of Pakistan and the other half to remain with India. Gandhi held that such a development, in which the two communities would have to work in cooperation, would make a positive contribution towards bringing different parts into a common federation again for the good of all.

Pursuing this logic, Gandhi conveyed to Jinnah that since he was now getting his Pakistan, it would be wise for him to speak to people of the Frontier as well as of East Punjab and West Bengal, to whichever party they might belong, and present his case in an attractive manner in the hope of being able to win them over to Pakistan. In pursuance of the same logic, Gandhi extended his support to the leaders of Bengal—where sentiments were strong to preserve the unity of common language, culture and ways of life—to keep Bengal undivided, independent of India and Pakistan. He similarly supported the demand of the Khan brothers in the Frontier Province that the Muslims and Hindus of that province should be given the choice to vote for independence as well instead of voting either for Pakistan or India. "There has been a growing demand in the (Frontier) Province for independence," wrote Congress President Kripalani to the Viceroy. "The proposed referendum should provide for the people voting for independence and subsequent decision as to their relation with the rest of India."[19]

Unknown to Gandhi and the Congress President, Nehru had, however, already taken away that option from the scheme of partition. "Mr. Kripalani's letter puts forward once more the suggestion," wrote Mountbatten to Nehru, "of allowing the Frontier to vote for independence ... I have not of course made the point in ... reply that it was at your written request that the option for Provinces to vote for independence was taken out, and that Mr. Jinnah (who was in favour of Bengal being allowed to vote for independence) is aware of the fact that I conceded this point to the Congress. But in the circumstances, you will see that both your position and my position would be completely untenable if either of us were to go back on this arrangement now."[20]

Bengal and the Frontier could, in the circumstances, vote for independence only if both the Congress and the Muslim League agreed to such a line of action. Jinnah, however, was opposed to the Frontier being allowed that option unless Bengal too had that freedom; Nehru and Patel were vehemently opposed to Bengal being allowed that option though they had no objection to the Frontier getting that freedom. In the event, the Khan brothers and the Congress in the Frontier boycotted the referendum and sadly allowed the Province to become part of Pakistan. And it took twenty-five years for the Pakistan part of Bengal to assert its linguistic and cultural identity to become independent of Pakistan.

* * *

The difference in approach and outlook between Gandhi and his colleagues in the Congress, which left them facing different directions on the eve of independence, was not confined to political issues alone; it extended to economic and social issues and values as well.

Gandhi was "opposed to the Congress fighting the elections with funds," Pyarelal had recorded. People knew, Gandhi held, who were their true servants; the Congressmen should, therefore, stand to be elected with the badge of their service on them alone. He was opposed also to putting up of any individual merely to derive diplomatic advantage against the opponent. "His advice was not followed" by the Congress in the elections for Central and Provincial Assemblies in the winter of 1945-46. One such candidate who was funded by the Congress to oppose the Muslim League was Ghularo Sarwar who later, in 1946, masterminded the Noakhali riots.[21]

Gandhi's advice was neither Utopian nor impractical. It is as valid and practical today as it was more than half a century ago. A writer had told us, through the columns of a national daily, that V. P. Singh got elected to Parliament by spending next to nothing. He nursed his constituency and the constituency had been electing him to Parliament. V. P. Singh had been once the Prime Minister of India too.

In years to come, the Congress turned itself into a mighty election machine. It raised and spent colossal amounts on elections. It sought and received big donations as the ruling party from trade and industry.

There was a time when candidates campaigned on bicycles and won elections, wrote M. N. Buch, a former civil servant. They did not have to purchase space to advertise or display banners and posters in a big way. But now they receive and spend often in millions. "A good candidate who is known to the people does not have to purchase attention or buy votes. It is only the political buffoons, who spend money not only to buy votes but to purchase power."

"Having accustomed to being in power for long spells," the Congressmen forgot that "votes not leaders put them there," wrote V. N. Narayanan in *Hindustan Times*. "In their conviction that their victory in elections depended ... more on money and muscle power than on grassroots support, more on manipulation than on established reputation for integrity and service," they sought vote banks instead of votes and shamelessly promoted "divisive identities in terms of religion, caste, language, whatever."

"I want to write about difference of outlook between us," Gandhi had written to Nehru two years before independence. "If the difference is fundamental then ... the public should be ... made aware of it. It would be detrimental to our work ... to keep them in the dark ... I want our position vis-à-vis each other to be clearly understood by us ... The bond that unites us is not only political ... I am now an old man. I have, therefore, named you as my heir. I must, however, understand my heir and my heir should understand me."

"I am convinced," wrote Gandhi in his letter, "that if India is to attain true freedom and through India the world also, then sooner or later the fact must be recognised that the people will have to live in villages not in towns, in huts not in palaces. Crores of people will never be able to live at peace with each other in towns and palaces. They will then have no recourse but to resort to both violence and untruth."

"You must not imagine," Gandhi went on to explain, "that I am envisaging our village life as it is today ... My ideal village will contain intelligent human beings. They will not live in dirt and darkness ... Men and women will be free and able to hold their own against anyone in the world."

"The essence of what I have said is," Gandhi concluded, "that man should rest content with what are his real needs ... We can realise truth and non-violence only in the simplicity of village life ... I must not fear if the world today is going the wrong way. It may be that India too will go that way and like the proverbial moth burn itself eventually in the flames round which it dances more and more fiercely. But it is my bounded duty up to my last breath to try to protect India and through India the entire world from such a doom."[22]

This had brought the following from Nehru in reply about people having to live in villages not in towns, in huts not in palaces: "I do not understand why a village should necessarily embody truth and non-violence. A village, normally speaking, is backward intellectually and culturally, and no progress can be made from a backward environment ... There is no question of palaces for millions of people. But there seems to be no reason why millions should not have comfortable up-to-date homes where they can lead a cultured existence."[23]

Nehru obviously missed the point that the Indian villages were in the condition that they were, was the direct result of the long British rule in India.

Gandhi in his letter to Nehru had stated, too, that "you must not imagine that I am envisaging our village life as it is today ... My ideal village will contain intelligent human beings ... They will not live in dirt and darkness."

* * *

Writing in his book *The Third Wave* more than three decades after Gandhi's assassination, Alvin Toffler, a former Associate Editor of *Fortune*, who served as visiting professor at Cornell University and taught at the New School for Social Research, stated that as the Industrial Revolution was coming to a close, it "left behind a world in which one quarter" of the population "lived in relative affluence, three-quarters in relative poverty—800,000,000 in what the World Bank terms 'absolute poverty.' Fully 700,000,000 people were underfed ... An estimated 1,200,000,000 human beings remained without access to public health facilities or ... even safe, drinkable water ... ."

Since the late 1940s, says Toffler, a "a single dominant strategy has governed most efforts to reduce the gap between the world's rich and poor ..." This strategy started "with the premise" that the societies based on the Industrial Revolution "are the apex of evolutionary progress and that, to solve their problems, all societies must replay the Industrial Revolution essentially as it happened in the West, the Soviet Union or Japan. Progress consists of moving millions of people out of agriculture into mass production. It requires urbanisation, standardisation ... in brief ... faithful imitation of an already successful model. Scores of Governments in country after country have ... tried to carry out this game plan ... but most such efforts have met with disaster. These failures in one impoverished country after another have been blamed on a mind bending multiplicity of reasons ... Yet, whatever the reasons, the grim fact remains that industrialisation ... model has flopped far more frequently than it has succeeded."

Citing the case of Iran, where the Shah as late as in 1975 "boasted he would make Iran into the most advanced industrial state in the Middle East" by pursuing the Industrial Revolution blueprint of the West, Toffler quotes *Newsweek* reporting that while "the Shah's builders toiled over a glorious array of mills, dams, railroads, highways and all the other trimmings of a full-fledged Industrial Revolution," which was supposedly turning Iran into a modern nation, "corruption ruled Teheran. Conspicuous consumption aggravated the contrast between rich and poor ... Apart from oil, fully two-thirds of all the goods produced for the market were consumed in Teheran by one-tenth the country's population. In the countryside ... the rural masses continued to live under revolting conditions."

The Indian scene was not very different.

The international agencies such as the World Bank, and many of the developing countries consequently had to reevaluate and revise the developmental strategy. "Instead of squeezing the peasants and forcing them into overburdened cities," says Toffler, the new strategy called for developmental activities in a rural setting. "Instead of concentrating on cash crops for export, it urges food selfsufficiency. Instead of striving blindly for higher GNP in the hopes that benefits will trickle down to the poor, it calls for resources to be channelled directly into basic human needs."

"There is much about this new formula that admittedly makes excellent sense," Toffler comments. "It confronts the need to slow down the massive migration to the cities. It aims to make the villages—where the bulk of the world's poor dwell—more liveable. It is sensitive to the ecological factors. It stresses the use of cheap local resources rather than expensive imports. It challenges conventional, all-too-narrow definitions of 'efficiency.' It suggests a less technocratic approach to development, taking local custom and culture into account. It emphasises improving the conditions of the poor rather than passing capital through the hands of the rich in the hopes that some will trickle down."

Gandhi was not saying anything different several decades earlier.

An Indian "futurist writer," who had "turned ten arid, miserably unproductive acres into a world-renowned model 'solar farm' with a biogas plant" producing "enough grains, fruits, and vegetables to feed his family and employees as well as tons of food to sell at a profit to the marketplace," says Toffler, "has written that a new 'balance has now to be struck between'—the most advanced science and technology available to the human race and 'the Gandhian vision of the idyllic green pastures, the village republics.' Such a practical combination ... requires a 'total transformation of the society, its symbols and values, its system of education, its incentives, the flow of its energy resources, its scientific and industrial research and a whole lot of other institutions."

Records Toffler: "An increasing number of long-range thinkers, social analysts, scholars, and scientists believe that just such a transformation ... towards a radical new synthesis: Gandhi ... with satellites" has become essential and is "now under way."

* * *

After independence had been achieved, Gandhi expected the rulers of independent India—the Congress leaders—to set an example of living a simple life in modest houses. "I feel that the Viceroy should be allowed to go to an unpretentious house and that the present palace should be more usefully used," advised Gandhi to Prime Minister-designate Nehru on the eve of transfer of power.[24] Therefore when Mountbatten offered to "move into a smaller house," in a letter to the Viceroy Gandhi "deeply ... appreciated" his desire "as the chosen Governor-General of the millions of the half-famished villagers," and hoped that "it would be possible to carry out" his wish.[25]

But that was not to be. Nehru expressed his reluctance to act on Gandhi's advice, pointing out the "difficulty in finding suitable accommodation and making arrangements for changing over, when we are so busy."[26] Recorded Pyarelal: "That could not have been the whole reason" because not only during Mountbatten's tenure but "even after the installation of the Indian Governor-General, no change was made either in the residence or the style of its upkeep."[27]

Mountbatten was, consequently, informed by Nehru that an immediate change over to a smaller house by the Viceroy would add to his difficulty. And not much later, Nehru himself moved from his modest abode on York Road (present-day Motilal Nehru Marg) to the house of the Commander-in-Chief, next in grandeur only to the Viceroy's House. As time passed, this also gradually became the model and norm—not austere but ostentatious living, not modest houses but the bigger the better—for the rulers of independent India.

The malady took deeper roots as the years went by. The Committee on Prevention of Corruption in its report in 1964 recorded that "there is a widespread impression that failure of integrity is not uncommon among Ministers and that some Ministers who have held office during the last sixteen years have enriched themselves illegitimately ... (and) reaped other advantages inconsistent with any notion of purity in public life ..."

It is said that during Chandragupta Maurya's rule in Pataliputra, looking for his well-known Minister Chanakya, a foreigner was directed to a riverside hut. Asked why he lived in a modest hut when people in the magnificent Pataliputra lived prosperously, Chanakya in his characteristic style is said to have replied that when rulers lived in palatial houses, people are condemned to live in huts.

One does not have to go far to comprehend the significance of Gandhi's advice and Chanakya's remarks. After almost half a century of attaining independence, India has yet to find and provide modest huts to its millions; for them "comfortable up-to-date homes" of Nehru's concept must therefore continue to remain only an unattainable Utopia. It had been estimated by the National Building Organisation that the shortage of housing in India at the beginning of 1991 was of the order of 30 million units, which was expected to increase to 40 million by the turn of the century. "Most people cannot afford to build a house," G. C. Mathur, a former Director of the National Building Organisation, noted. "Over half of the population in metropolitan centres and large cities is living in slums ... whereas vast majority of rural people are living in dilapidated homes."

* * *

With growing concern Gandhi noted the change that had come over the leaders from the ideals which the Congress had preached, cherished and upheld in the past. Nothing escaped his watchful eye. A news item which reported that a Cabinet Minister had requested for a new set of furniture for his official residence, and that the Indian ambassadors were asking for large sums towards furnishing and entertainment, disturbed Gandhi. He drew Nehru's attention to it.[28] He was told in reply that "the press message is largely untrue or greatly exaggerated," and that the British pound "having fallen in value, does not buy as much as it used to." Gandhi, however, "continued to note with growing uneasiness the unchecked administrative waste and lavish expenditure when millions were suffering untold hardships."[28] In a letter to Nehru he cautioned: "We are going in for British extravagance which the country cannot afford."[29]

Reviewing a biography of Nehru, a discerning writer has stated that "Nehru without power" was "a disciple of Gandhi" but "with power" he was "a broker of Western civilisation." He was "charming ... sensitive, a deep thinker, humanitarian, liberal, democrat ... and a dreamer." But what "remained of his relationship with Gandhi was one of attachment only" and not that of an inheritor of Gandhi's political or economic philosophy.[30]

In common with Thomas Jefferson, one of the outstanding Presidents of the USA, Gandhi considered binding and saddling coming generations with debt as unauthorised and immoral. He wanted the Government to manage within the resources available to it. His warning of course went unheeded. The result may be found in the unprecedented national debt that independent India has accumulated over the years, and which in the year 1994 stood at a staggering 470,000 crores of rupees, the annual debt service or interest payment on which, according to Nani Palkhivala, aggregated to Rs. 46,000 crore or 53 per cent of the revenue receipt of the Government of India for the year.

The World Bank reported that India's external debt in 1993 touched a record of $292 billion, making it the third largest debtor next only to Brazil and Mexico among the developing countries. However in a convoluted way of looking at things, it had been explained that even so one should not assume that India was in the middle of a debt-trap, while admitting at the same time that the debt contained some of the factors that fuelled the currency crisis resulting in Mexico's economic collapse from which USA had to bale it out with massive financial support.

Fifteen years later, by the time this book went into its third edition in 2009, according to a newspaper report based on official information, the Central Government's public ... debt at the end of year 2008 has been increasing in absolute terms, on account of persistent fiscal deficit, which in turn is financed by both internal and external borrowing of the Government. The country's external debt at the end of June 2008 stood at Rs. 20,65,600 crores, and the outstanding internal debt stood at Rs. 29,39,237 crores, up from Rs. 16,90,554 crores in the year 2003-2004.

* * *

Gandhi felt deeply worried and concerned too over the growing "scrambles for loaves and fishes" in the Congress and the "personal rivalries" among the Congress leaders. A crisis situation developed between the titans of the Congress leadership. Matters came to a head within four months of the formation of the Government of free India. The Sardar took exception to Nehru sending an officer as his representative to a place which was under Sardar's charge without taking Patel into confidence. Exchange of letters followed leading to Nehru conveying to Gandhi that Patel should leave the Cabinet unless he accepted the special position of the PM, or he himself should go out.

"I think that my sending him was ... completely within my competence," said Nehru in his note to Gandhi on January 6, 1948, less than a month before the Mahatma's assassination. "Is the PM entitled to take such a step and who is to be the judge of this? If the PM ... is not himself to be judge of what is proper and what is not in such matters, then he should cease to be PM."

"The recent correspondence between Sardar Patel and me has raised important issues of vital consequences," wrote Nehru in his note to Gandhi. "It is true that there are not only temperamental differences between Sardar and me but also differences in approach in respect to economic and communal matters ... Nevertheless ... there was obviously a very great deal in common in addition to mutual respect and affection and ... the same national political aim of freedom. Because of this we functioned together during all these years and did our utmost to adapt ourselves to each other ... ."

"Our political aim having been more or less achieved," said Nehru in his note, "the other question, on which we have differed to some extent, comes more and more to the forefront." However, leaving out of consideration these important matters for the moment, said Nehru, "we may ... come down to the immediate issue. This issue essentially relates to the functions of the Prime Minister. It is something much more than a personal issue and it should be considered, therefore, as a question of principle, whoever the PM might be."

"But whatever the theory may be," Nehru went on to add, "practical difficulties continually arise ... After having given serious thought to this matter I have come to the conclusion that as far as possible we must avoid, at this particular juncture, any parting of ways in the Government ... At the same time I do feel that the Prime Minister's function ... must be appreciated. If, however, this is not considered possible, then the only alternative left is for either me or Sardar Patel to leave the Cabinet ... I consider this an undesirable alternative in the present context and I have come to this conclusion as objectively as possible. If someone has to leave, I repeat, I would prefer to leave."

Nehru passed on a copy of his note to Sardar Patel, suggesting that they both may meet at Gandhi's place for a further talk on this subject. In reply Sardar Patel sent to Nehru a copy of his note that he had sent to Gandhi on receipt of Nehru's note.

"There is no disagreement on the existence of temperamental differences and different outlook on economic matters and those affecting Hindu-Muslim relations," said Sardar Patel in his note to Gandhi. "Both of us, however, place the interests of the country above these personal differences and, aided by mutual regard, respect and love for each other, have cooperated in a common endeavour. Through our joint efforts we have weathered many a storm ... and got over one of the most critical phases in the history of any country ... It is painful and rather tragic to reflect that we cannot carry this any further; but I fully realise the strength of feeling and conviction behind the Prime Minster's stand as regards his own position.

"I have tried my best to appreciate what he says on the subject ... on the twin basis of democracy and Cabinet responsibility (but) found myself unable to agree with his conception of the Prime Minister's duties and responsibilities. That conception, if accepted, would raise the Prime Minister to the position of a virtual dictator, for he claims full freedom to act when and how he chooses. This in my opinion is wholly opposed to democratic and Cabinet system of government."

The Sardar put on record that "the Prime Minister's position, according to my conception, is certainly pre-eminent; he is first among equals. But he has no over-riding powers over his colleagues; if he had any, a Cabinet and Cabinet responsibility would be superfluous ... The Prime Minister, as the leader of the party and the head of the whole administration, is inevitably concerned that Cabinet decisions are effective ... He has accordingly the right to ask for information from the Minister concerned, as well as the right to consult and advise on the lines of policy to be adopted and even the manner in which the policy is to be implemented ... This position of the Prime Minister not only fully safeguards his pre-eminence and makes him an effective head of the administration but is also fully in accord with democratic principles and rules of Ministerial and Cabinet responsibility."

With regard to sending an officer by Nehru to Ajmer, to which Sardar had taken exception, he was unable "to share the Prime Minister's view of its nature or its consequences ... It was not that I did not want anyone to go. When the Prime Minister mentioned to me that he wanted to go, I promptly agreed that he should go. I did not come to know of Iengar's visit in substitution of the Prime Minister's until after Iengar had returned ... The question is not whether the Prime Minister was entitled to take the step or not or whether he is not to be the judge of the propriety or the action but whether I, as a Minister, was wrong in pointing out to him the inadvisability of the course he had taken and the probable consequences it entailed."

The Sardar ended his note with the following statement: "The Prime Minister has also referred to his preference for leaving office if mutual accommodation cannot be secured. I maintain, however, that if anybody has to go, it should be myself. I have passed the age of active service. The Prime Minister is the acknowledged leader of the country and is comparatively young; he has established an international position of pre-eminence for himself. I have no doubt that the choice between him and myself should be resolved in his favour. Therefore, there is no question of his quitting office."

Gandhi felt unhappy at the turn of events. He was of the view that the larger national interest required both the leaders to work in harmony as close colleagues not withstanding temperamental and other differences between them, and means have to be devised to make it possible. He decided to meet Nehru and Patel together to thrash out an acceptable solution. This was however delayed due to the fast he had undertaken to bring back the communal harmony in Delhi.

* * *

Gandhi's uneasiness with all that was taking place in independent India was palpable. Four days before his assassination, Gandhi gave expression to his deep frustration in his after-prayer speech. "This day, January 26, is Independence Day," said Gandhi in his speech. "This observance was quite appropriate when we were fighting for independence we had not seen or handled. Now we have handled it and seem to be disillusioned. At least I am even if you are not ... We are entitled to celebrate the hope ... that we are on the road to showing the lowliest of the village that it means his freedom from serfdom and that he is the salt of the Indian earth. Let us not defer the hope and make the heart sick."

On another occasion he said: There was a time when India listened to him. Today he was a back number. He was told that he had no place in the new order. If they could have the courage to say that they would retain freedom with the help of the same force with which they had won it, he was their man. His physical incapacity and his depression would vanish in a moment.

Although deeply distressed and worried at the spread of communal violence from Calcutta to Noakhali to Bihar, in the course of a few months during later half of 1946, Gandhi had not felt "depressed" or "disillusioned." He accepted the challenge and continued to aspire to live for 125 years, if God willed him to continue to serve the humanity.

Less than a year earlier in January 1947, in a letter to Satis Mukerji, a reference about whom has been made in the Introduction to this book, Gandhi wrote to him that "I would love to think that you will finish your full span of 125 years, which I may not do for want of equanimity prescribed in the concluding verses of the Gita ... I am trying hard to reach that stage."

The reasons that led to Gandhi's "disillusionment" and "depression" to which he had began to give frequent expression by the end of the year, is therefore to be searched and found somewhere else. He had been unable to prevent partition of the country, which he had considered a tragedy and a disaster, with his close colleagues choosing a different route against his advice and pleadings. And independent India had taken a different road too than what Gandhi had envisaged and expected them to follow, for which the path had become all the more smoother, with no real opposition to Congress left after partition for the leadership to travel that road These were then the reasons that made Gandhi feel the way he had begun to express himself repeatedly during those last weeks and days of his life. And even though he had mentioned only a few months earlier that he was "trying hard" to achieve the required equanimity to attain the age of 125 years, he now began to feel that he may not be able to sustain the equanimity as a result of "disillusionment" and "depression." He often told that he did not want to live upto 125 years. On his 78th birthday he told his visitors that "I do not wish another birthday to overtake me in an India still in flames."

* * *

Events were however taking different turn in the meanwhile. A bomb exploded at the site of his evening prayer meeting giving an indication of the shape of things to come. A group of Hindus got enraged at his undertaking fast to protect Muslims of Delhi, when unprecedented carnage was the order of the day all over Punjab with Hindu refugees in hundreds and thousands pouring in on the Indian side of the border, bringing with them the tale of horrible suffering that they had to undergo.

Meeting with Nehru and Patel to sort out their differences had been delayed. "I mentioned this matter to him and he said that we might postpone the discussion for a little while till certain immediate and urgent issues had been dealt with," wrote Nehru to Sardar Patel.

On the fateful day—January 30,1948—soon after the fast was over as a result of complete restoration of peace in Delhi—and undertaking given by leaders of both communities to continue to maintain peace—a repeat of Calcutta, Gandhi decided to call Nehru and Patel on the next day—January 31—for the meeting. Sardar was the last person to meet Gandhi that afternoon, which delayed Gandhi's going to the evening prayer meeting, where the assassin Nathuram Godse was waiting to receive him with his three fatal bullets.

Gandhi's death resulted in the controversy between Nehru and Patel getting a decent burial. Gandhi sealed their friendship in his death. "When Bapu was alive we had hoped to meet him together and discuss various matters that had troubled us somewhat," wrote Nehru to Patel soon after Gandhi's assassination, signing his letter as "Your affectionately, Jawaharlal."

"In my last letter I had expressed the hope," Nehru went on to add, "that, in spite of certain differences of opinion and temperament, we should continue to pull together as we had done for so long. This was, I was glad to find, Bapu's final opinion also.

"It is over a quarter of a century since we have been closely associated with one another," Nehru went on to add, "and we have faced many storms and perils together. I can say with full honesty that during this period my affection and regard for you have grown, and I do not think anything can happen to lesson this. Even our differences have brought out the far greater points of agreement between us and the respect we bear to each other. We have even learnt to agree to differ and yet carry on together.

"Anyway, in the crisis that we have to (face) now after Bapu's death, I think it is my duty and, if I may venture to say yours also, for us to face it together as friends and colleagues. Not merely superficially, but in full loyalty to one another and with confidence in each other. I can assure you that you will have that from me. If I have any doubt or difficulty I shall put it frankly to you, and I hope you will do the same to me."

The Sardar was a changed man too. "I am deeply touched, indeed overwhelmed, by the affection and the warmth of your letter," replied Sardar to Nehru. "I fully and heartily reciprocate the sentiments you have so feelingly expressed.

"I had the good fortune to have a last talk with him for over an hour just before his death and he communicated to me what had passed between you and him ... His opinion also binds us both and I can assure you that I am fully resolved to approach my responsibilities and obligations in this spirit."

* * *

During the last months of his life Gandhi had turned his attention to the role that the Congress organisation should play in independent India. After deep consideration he came to the conclusion that the Congress in its existing form should dissolve itself before the rot set in further in that organisation. He therefore started devising a new constitution that would "enable the Congress effectively to complete the social revolution for which the independence of India had cleared the way ... and to guide the politics of the country instead of being reduced to the status of a mere party machine in the hands of the ruling group."[31]

"Though split into two, India having attained political independence ... the Congress in its present shape and form has outlived its use" read the preamble of the note Gandhi prepared a day before he was assassinated. But "India has still to attain social, moral and economic independence in terms of its villages as distinguished from its cities and towns." The Congress, therefore, "must be kept out of unhealthy competition with political parties ... and communal bodies" to work for the attainment of those goals. For these reasons, advised Gandhi in what became his last will and testament, the All-India Congress Committee should resolve "to disband the existing Congress organisation, and flower into a Lok Sevak Sangh."

Wanting nothing for himself ... knowing no jealousy, giving himself no airs, never scornful ... eager to believe the best, always hopeful, always patient, Gandhi hoped that the Congress leaders would accept his advice and transform the Congress to meet the bigger challenge that faced the country. The leaders were, however, in no mood to heed the Mahatma's advice, even when it was sealed and delivered to them with his supreme sacrifice. They put his advice quietly on the shelf. Instead of disbanding itself, the Congress changed its role from spearheading the national movement to achieve independence to that of a political party to control all the levers of power.

The Congress had drawn under its umbrella "elements with different political philosophies," a perceptive writer had noted, and what held them together was not a common ideology but a common desire for independence. The scenario envisaged by the Mahatma, in which the dissolution of the Congress would "lead to emergence of ideology-based strong political parties" did not take place. What took place instead was the Congress rule all over the country and the corrupting influence of unrivalled and unchecked power. The economic and social freedom of the masses for which Gandhi wanted the Congress to dedicate after disbanding itself, thus remained as distant a goal as ever.

Afterword

A few years after Gandhi's passing away, Nehru decided that the day of Gandhi's assassination, January 30, was to be observed each year as martyr's day, with President of India taking salute from an army contingent at Rajghat, where Gandhi's body was cremated, to be followed by booming of artillery gun at noon to observe a minute's silence by public in memory of the martyrs in general.

Gandhi's secretary Pyarelal along with Vinoba, whom Gandhi had chosen to be the first to offer civil disobedience against the gagging laws at the beginning of the Second World War in 1939, found themselves in disagreement to armed personnel lining up at Gandhi's Samadhi to present military salute to the President.

They with some of the like-minded people decided to make their opposition to the idea public and a statement to that effect was prepared and signed by them for release to the Press. It was decided that Pyarelal was to meet Nehru to give him a copy of the proposed statement before it was released to the Press.

Nehru told Pyarelal, when they met, that he was himself not very happy with the practice put in place, and was giving a second thought to the best possible way in which the practice of taking salute from army contingent at Mahatma's Samadhi could be discontinued. Pyarelal also reported Nehru telling him that he was not comfortable with the display of military might at the annual Republic Day parade that took place a few days earlier on 26 January, and would like it gradually to become a function/parade displaying the cultural diversity of different parts and regions of the country with minimum military display. The group therefore decided that in view of what Nehru himself was planning to do, their statement may not be made public.

However the practice of arm salute at Rajghat continued, not only during Nehru's lifetime but later as well.

* * *

After the explosion of a bomb at the site of Gandhi's evening prayer meeting in the compound of Birla House in New Delhi in January 1948, Home Minister Sardar Patel wanted people to be frisked before they were to be allowed entry to prayer ground. But Gandhi refused permission to do so. A commemorative prayer meeting is held each year in that place, now known as "Gandhi Smriti," but it is not open to the general public. The advertisement in the national daily announces that on "anniversary of the martyrdom of the father of the nation ... a commemorative prayer will be held at Gandhi Smriti. ... Admission by invitation only."

* * *

After achieving his goal of carving out a Muslim-majority State in two parts, separated by hundreds of miles of Indian territory, which left behind one-fourth of Muslim population in the remaining part of Indian sub-continent, and himself becoming Head of Pakistan, it did not take long for Jinnah to appear once again in a secular garb—a preacher of communal harmony between Hindus and Muslims and followers of other faiths living in the same country, as was the case earlier during his youth. But it was not an easy task now to achieve that goal when he had used every possible means in his last years to put asunder the beautiful mosaic of composite culture and unity of the Indian subcontinent to achieve his goal of Pakistan.

Addressing the Pakistan Constituent Assembly in Karachi on August 11, 1947, four days before the official birth of Pakistan, Jinnah had told the members of the Assembly that "you may belong to any religion or caste or creed—that has nothing to do with the business of the State ... In course of time Hindus would cease to be Hindus and Muslims would cease to be Muslims, not in religious sense because that is the personal faith of each individual, but in the political sense as the citizen of the State."

Jinnah was however left with not much time to get his wish translated into facts of life in Pakistan, even if he had so wished in the changed situation. Roderick Mathews in his book *"Jinnah Vs Gandhi"* recorded that "when given supreme power in Pakistan, with no higher authority above him, and no equals, when his long career of opportunity competition and minority status was finally behind him, he seemed bereft of purpose". He was by then a very sick man with terminal illness and passed away in less than fourteen months of the creation of Pakistan.

In his book *The Shadow of the Great Game*, Narendra Singh Sarila has quoted Col. Elahi Baksh, the physician who attended on Jinnah during his last illness in August-September of 1948, that he had heard Jinnah saying: "I have made it (Pakistan) but I am convinced that I have committed the greatest blunder of my life."And around the same period, after meeting Jinnah on his sick-bed, the Pakistan Prime Minister Liaquat Ali Khan was heard to have muttered: "The old man has now discovered his mistake."

* * *

If history is to be recorded, East Pakistan became an independent country of Bangla Desh after a bloody Civil War in less than twenty-five years of its creation in 1947.

In his book *Jinnah Vs Gandhi* Roderick Mathew also recorded that "Jinnah can still correctly be seen as the main instigator in the process that led to Pakistan, for if he had reached agreement with the Congress than the dynamic that led to Pakistan would have been altered or even avoided." However "it was Congress that pressed for Partition in the final days and that Jinnah was reluctant to accept the reality he had brought about".

Stating the other side of the story, the author recorded that "the British separately emphasized to Jinnah the weakness of any possible version of Pakistan, expecting him to refuse it. In the end he did not refuse, but hurtled away from the negotiating table by the Congress, who suddenly changed track. Having remained opposed to giving Jinnah anything like a sovereign state, Congress leaders suddenly showed the British the green light in April 1947.

The author goes on to record that " Gandhi ... never shared the concern for ego gratification to be found at the centre of so many political lives, including the Quaide Azam. When he went to offer the Interim Government to Jinnah in April 1947, he illustrated his full faith in full measure. He genuinely thought that to give Jinnah the supreme office was the best way to prove, definitely, that the Congress did not have an anti-muslim agenda ... Where he was mistaken was that his colleagues would simply never permit so drastic a concession ... Gandhi was aware of Jinnaha's probable reaction to his radical offer... The Mahatma understood many aspects of high political strategy but his instinct led him to placate his declared opponent to show how little he cared for power... "Gandhi was the great unifying force in the congress politics. Congress under Gandhi stayed together by not being too strictly led ... He was mainly a moral force for unity. Although he had no official position in the Congress in 1942, it was to him that the authority to launch the Quit India campaign in 1942 was designated. Congress politicians themselves considered his guidance to be indispensable up until 1947."

༂

Facsimile of Gandhi's Letter to President Roosevelt

Sevagram, Via. Wardha
(India)
1st July 1942

Dear Friend,

I twice missed coming to your great country. I have the privilege of having numerous friends there both known and unknown to me. Many of my countrymen have received and are still receiving higher education in America. I know too that several have taken shelter there. I have profited greatly by the writings of Thoreau and Emerson. I say this to tell you how much I am connected with your country. Of Great Britain I need say nothing beyond mentioning that in spite of my intense dislike of British Rule, I have numerous personal friends in England whom I love as dearly as my own people. I had my legal education there. I have therefore nothing but good wishes for your country and Great Britain. You will therefore accept my word that my present proposal, that the British should unreservedly and without reference to the wishes of the people of India immediately withdraw their rule, is prompted by the friendliest intention. I would like to turn into goodwill the ill will which, whatever may be said to the contrary, exists in India towards Great Britain and thus enable the millions of India to play their part in the present war.

My personal position is clear. I hate all war. If, therefore, I could persuade my countrymen, they would make a most effective and decisive contribution in favour of an honourable peace. But I know that all of us have not a living faith in non-violence. Under foreign rule however we can make no effective contribution of any kind in this war, except as helots.

The policy of the Indian National Congress, largely guided by me, has been one of non-embarrassment to Britain, consistently with the honourable working of the Congress, admittedly the largest political organisation, of the longest standing in India. The British policy as exposed by the Cripps mission and rejected by almost all parties has opened our eyes and has driven me to the proposal I have made. I hold that the full acceptance of my proposal and that alone can put the Allied cause on an unassailable basis. I venture to think that the Allied declaration that the Allies are fighting to make the world safe for freedom of the individual and for democracy sounds hollow, so long as India and, for that matter, Africa are exploited by Great Britain, and America has the Negro problem in her own home. But in order to avoid all complications, in my proposal I have confined myself only to India. If India becomes free the rest must follow, if it does not happen simultaneously.

In order to make my proposal foolproof I have suggested that, if the Allies think it necessary, they may keep their troops, at their own expense, in India, not for keeping internal order but for preventing Japanese aggression and defending China. So far as India is concerned, we must become free even as America and Great Britain are. The Allied troops will remain in India during the war under treaty with the free India Government that may be formed by the people of India without any outside interference, direct or indirect.

It is on behalf of this proposal that I write this to enlist your active sympathy.

I hope that it would commend itself to you.

Mr. Louis Fischer is carrying this letter to you.

If there is any obscurity in my letter, you have but to send me word and I shall try to clear it.

I hope finally that you will not resent this letter as an intrusion but take it as an approach from a friend and well-wisher of the Allies.

I remain,
Yours sincerely,
M. K. Gandhi

President Franklin D. Roosevelt

(Courtesy: Franklin D. Roosevelt Library)

*Mahatma Gandhi at Sodepur Ashram.
D.C. Jha in the background*

Appendix 1

Gandhi's Last Will and Testament

Though split into two, India having attained political independence through means devised by the Indian National Congress, the Congress in its present shape and form, i.e., as a propaganda vehicle and parliamentary machine, has outlived its use. India has still to attain social, moral and economic independence in terms of its seven hundred thousand villages as distinguished from its cities and towns. The struggle for the ascendancy of civil over military power is bound to take place in India's progress towards it democratic goal. It must be kept out of unhealthy competition with political parties and communal bodies. For these and other similar reasons, the AICC resolves to disband the existing Congress organisation and flower into a Lok Sevak Sangh under the following rules with power to alter them as the occasion may demand.

Every Panchayat of five adult men or women being villagers or village-minded shall form a unit.

Two such contiguous Panchayats shall form a working party under a leader elected from among themselves.

When there are one hundred such Panchayats, the fifty first grade leaders shall elect from among themselves a second grade leader and so on, the first grade leaders meanwhile working under the second grade leader. Parallel groups of two hundred Panchayats shall continue to be formed till they cover the whole of India, each succeeding group of Panchayats electing second grade leader after the manner of the first. All second grade leaders shall serve jointly for the whole of India and severally for their respective areas. The second grade leaders may elect, whenever they deem necessary, from among themselves a chief who will, during pleasure, regulate and command all the groups.

(As the final formation of Provinces or districts is still in a state of flux, no attempt has been made to divide this group of servants into Provincial or District Councils and jurisdiction over the whole of India has been vested in the group or groups that may have been formed at any given time. It should be noted that this body of servants derive their authority or power from service ungrudgingly and wisely done to their master, the whole of India.)

1. Every worker shall be a habitual wearer of Khadi made from self-spun yarn or certified by the AISA and must be a teetotaller. If a Hindu he must have abjured untouchability in any shape or form in his own person or in his family and must be a believer in the ideal of inter-communal unity, equal respect and regard for all religions and equality of opportunity and status for all irrespective of race, creed or sex.
2. He shall come in personal contact with every villager within his jurisdiction.
3. He shall enrol and train workers from amongst the villagers and keep a register of all these.
4. He shall keep a record of his work from day to day.
5. He shall organise the villages so as to make them self-contained and self-supporting through their agriculture and handicrafts.
6. He shall educate the village folk in sanitation and hygiene and take all measures for prevention of ill health and disease among them.
7. He shall organise the education of the village folk from birth to death along the lines of Nai Talim, in accordance with the policy laid down by the Hindustani Talimi Sangh.
8. He shall see that those whose names are missing on the statutory voter's roll are duly entered therein.
9. He shall encourage those who have not yet acquired the legal qualification to acquire it for getting the right of franchise.
10. For the above purposes and others to be added from time to time, he shall train and fit himself in accordance with the rules laid down by the Sangh for the due performance of duty.

The Sangh shall affiliate the following autonomous bodies:
1. All-India Spinners' Association
2. All-India Village Industries Association
3. Hindustani Talimi Sangh
4. Harijan Sevak Sangh
5. Go-Seva Sangh

Finance:
The Sangh shall raise finances for the fulfilment of its mission from among the villagers and others, special stress being laid on collection of poor man's pice.

M. K. Gandhi
New Delhi, 29 January 1948

Appendix 2

Exchange of Letters

1. Gandhi to Satis Mukerji

Srirampur
Noakhali
9.12.1946

Dear Satis Babu,

Did Krishnadas tell you about the very silly mistake I made, viz., that you had gone to your rest? How I came to have that impression I cannot make out except for the fact that I had not heard from you for a long time. You can therefore imagine my joy when he told me that you were very much alive, were able to have regular walks and were able to give instruction to true seekers as usual. I would love to think that you will finish your full span of 125 years which I may not do for want of the equanimity prescribed in the concluding verses of the Gita, our Kamdhenu. I am trying hard to reach that stage. Do please write to me when you have the time.

Yours,

M. K. Gandhi

2. Satis Mukerji to Gandhi

Banaras City
24.1.1947

Revered Bapuji,

It ill becomes me to trouble you now, when you are immersed in the work of tackling and solving, if possible, an all-India problem, with an expression of my detailed views on the subject matter of your letter, dated Srirampur, Noakhali 9.12.46. Nevertheless I propose to write to you in outline about my view that longevity can be prolonged indefinitely, if only the utterance of Ram Nam (the Lord's Name) becomes with the Sadhak, not an act of conscious will or choice, but gets to be an automatic, inward process, springing from within and expressing itself outwardly, consciously or subconsciously. This in my view is only possible when the utterance of the Lord's name gets tacked on to, or better becomes a part of, the Sadhak's breathing movement.

Therefore, my second point is that the Lord's name or Ram Nam is no mere outer sound emitted by the Sadhak but is verily a form of spiritual or Divine Energy.

My third point is that when the utterance of Ram Nam gets to be intimately associated with the breathing movement of the Sadhak, it is bound to react on the whole of the Sadhak's external system, including the mental apparatus, scripturally known as the Linga-Sariram or Sukshma Sariram.

My fourth point is that when the spiritual or Chit Energy of the Divine thus reacts, then the whole apparatus Sthul (gross) and Sukshma (fine) gets to be impregnated with the Spiritual or Chit energy derived from or inhering in Ram Nam. Therefore, when that happens, what is to us at present material (whether of the grosser or the finer variety) becomes so energised by the Chit or Spiritual energy (which is of the essence of Ram Nam) that the laws of matter manifesting themselves in material disintegration and decay become, for the time being, suspended so to say. As the result of such suspension, the Sadhak could go on subsisting on the objective plane as an objective entity immune from the operation of forces which tend towards disintegration and decay.

Lastly and fifthly, at this stage, equanimity, a term which you have used, cannot be termed mental, i.e., born of the control of the mindstuff. Then it comes to be a function of the Sadhak's soul life and may therefore be called soul born. At this stage, the equanimity in question comes to be natural, deep and spontaneous.

The above point may be made clearer by saying that the type of equanimity which comes to be born of the process of utterance of Ram Nam, along with every exhalation and inhalation of the Sadhak's breath, far transcends in its very nature the kind of equanimity of which we can at present conceive. The reason for it, as already pointed out, is that the type of equanimity in question is no longer mindhom, but is essentially an offspring of soul life or spirituality. This higher type of equanimity is scripturally termed "Shanti." Of this type of "Shanti" there are higher and higher grades, of which the Gita speaks, e.g. Gita IV-39 (Parashanti) and V-12 (Naisthiki Shanti).

Your sincerely,

Satis Mukerji

3. Gandhi to Satis Mukerji

Dear Satis Babu,   Date: 1.2.1947

Your lovely letter, I endorse all your propositions, though probably I would put them differently and comprise them into one. But that does not diminish the value of the propositions. Alas I am far as yet from that state. At the same time I am hastening towards it. If I attain that state or even come near enough to it (and probably that is all that a human being can reach) this problem of Noakhali will be easily solved. Let us see what happens.

    Please do not hesitate to write to me or dictate a letter for me, whenever you feel like telling me something. Know that your messages will never be a strain on me.

Yours sincerely,

M. K. Gandhi

4. Dr. Rajendera Prasad to Satis Mukerji

1, Queen Victoria Road
New Delhi.
The 5th June, 1947

My dear Sir,

The other day I was in Calcutta just for a few hours and I happened to meet Deva Chandra who showed me the correspondence relating to a manuscript of an essay on non-violence which I had written in 1930 when I had the privilege of being with you at my village Ziradei. I had mentioned the matter in my Atma-Katha but I never imagined that it would be the cause of so much trouble to you, particularly at your age and with your naturally feeble health. I am, therefore, very sorry that you have been put to so much trouble. I am glad, however, that it has opened the way for this letter. I have not yet received the manuscript or its typed copy which Deva Chandra told me had not reached. I would ask you not to worry any more about it and let it come in due course, without taking any particular trouble about it.

I hope, your health, in spite of your age, is good. I am keeping fairly well, particularly during the hot weather when I ordinarily maintain good health.

You must be following the political developments that have taken place from day to day. Events are moving very fast and we hope that by August next, we shall get what is called "Dominion Status" which is said to be more or less equivalent to independence. As the Viceroy said yesterday at the press conference, HMG will not appoint any Governor-General at present in the service of the Government of India. But the country is said to be divided and not only the country as a whole but also the two provinces of Punjab and Bengal. It is an irony of time that the very people who fought against the partition of Bengal and got it reversed should now demand that it should be divided and that demand should be conceded just as the demand for the reversal of partition had to be conceded. But there was a more or less unanimous demand from Bengal Hindus and so far as I know, Sjt. Sarat Chandra Bose was practically isolated. So now we are going to enter into a momentous period of our history, i.e., to run it according to our own notions and ideas. There are, of course, limitations and inhibitions arising out of past history. Let us pray that God give us wisdom and strength to do the work honestly and diligently.

With kind regards.

Yours Sincerely,

Rajendra Prasad

5. Satis Mukerji to Dr. Rajendra Prasad

180, Ramapura,
Banaras City

My dear Rajendra Prasad,

Your letter of the 5th instant. My health is on the downgrade, but I am still carrying on. I shall not worry over your manuscript about which I had completely forgotten, until I learnt something about it from Deva Chandra's father, who sent me some extracts from what you had written about it in your Atma-Katha. Even then, after a lapse of some sixteen or seventeen years, it was hardly possible for me to lay my hands on your manuscript, stowed away among a heap of forgotten things. Most fortunately for me, a friend of mine came to my rescue; and he it was, and not I myself, who discovered it for me. Only one page of the manuscript however, is missing. Looking through it, I found that I had done my work very carefully indeed, although I don't know whether you will be in a position to accept my views, such as they are, which I had jotted down towards the close of your manuscript.

My health is on the downgrade, my present age being eighty-three running. My legs are feeble, but I am enjoined to have regular, short walks, which I do by resting my hand on the shoulder of a kind friend. The lower limbs of the body have deteriorated but the rest of the body is quite fit. I spend most of my time in reading and writing; much in the way I used to do when I was in my fifties. Pujya Mahatmaji has blessed me in a way, for his hope is that, under God's Grace, I should be able to carry on till I have "finished my full span of 125 years." To this hope he gave expression in a letter dated Noakhali, 9.12.46.

But the main theme of your letter relates to the present political developments in the country. My view of the matter, however, is pessimistic. I fear that the centrifugal tendencies in the country are too strong to be brought under, if of course the present authorities choose to leave the country, as they assure us that they are going to do. For it seems to me that the solution of all other Indian problems relating to the well-being of the masses must wait till this primary one could be successfully tackled, and if possible, solved. I am one of those who are not very hopeful that the transfer of political power would be quite a peaceful affair. I pray, therefore, with yourself that "God will give us wisdom and strength to do our work honestly and diligently." But let me tell you that, from my point of view, the period ahead is a very strenuous one; and if the country is able to settle down within say the next three, four or even five years after the transfer of power has been formally affected, India will have indeed cause to rejoice.

I have said that we must all join in your prayer to the Almighty. Let us all pray that He may set India on her feet as early as possible. But we must not forget what on the very eve of His crucifixion Jesus said, while praying:

"Father, if Thou be willing, remove this cup from me. Nevertheless, not my will but Thine be done."

With love and respect,

Yours sincerely

S. C. Mukerji

Appendix 3

British Prime Minister's Statement Regarding Transfer of Power by June 1948

It has long been the policy of successive British Governments to work towards the realisation of self-government in India. In pursuance of this policy an increasing measure of responsibility has been devolved on Indians and today the civil administration and the Indian armed forces rely to a very large extent on Indian civilians and officers. In the constitutional field the Acts of 1919 and 1935 passed by the British Parliament each represented a substantial transfer of political power. In 1940 the Coalition Government recognised the principle that Indians should them selves frame a new constitution for a fully autonomous India, and in the offer of 1942 they invited them to set up a Constituent Assembly for this purpose as soon as the war was over.

His Majesty's Government believe this policy to have been right and in accordance with sound democratic principles. Since they came into office, they have done their utmost to carry it forward to its fulfilment. The declaration of the Prime Minister of March 15th last which met with general approval in Parliament and the country, made it clear that it was for the Indian people themselves to choose their future status and constitution and that in the opinion of His Majesty's Government the time had come for responsibility for the Government of India to pass into Indian hands.

The Cabinet Mission which was sent to India last year spent over three months in consultation with Indian leaders in order to help them to agree upon a method for determining the future constitution of India, so that the transfer of power might be smoothly and rapidly effected. It was only when it seemed clear that without some initiative from the Cabinet Mission agreement was unlikely to be reached that they put forward proposals themselves.

These proposals, made public in May last, envisaged that the future constitution of India should be settled by a Constituent Assembly composed, in the manner suggested therein, of representatives of all communities and interests in British India and of the Indian states.

Since the return of the Mission an Interim Government has been set up at the Centre composed of the political leaders of the major communities exercising wide powers within the existing constitution. In the Provinces Indian Governments responsible to legislatures are in office.

It is with great regret that His Majesty's Government find that there are still differences among Indian parties which are preventing the Constituent Assembly from functioning as it was intended that it should. It is of the essence of the plan that the Assembly should be fully representative.

His Majesty's Government desire to hand over their responsibility to authorities established by a constitution approved by all parties in India in accordance with the Cabinet Mission's plan, but unfortunately there is at present no prospect that such a constitution and such authorities will emerge. The present state of uncertainty is fraught with danger and cannot be indefinitely prolonged. His Majesty's Government wish to make it clear that it is their definite intention to take the necessary steps to effect the transference of power into responsible Indian hands by a date not later than June 1948.

This great subcontinent now containing over 400 million people has for the last century enjoyed peace and security as part of the British Commonwealth and Empire. Continued peace and security are more than ever necessary today if the full possibilities of economic development are to be realised and a higher standard of life attained by the Indian people.

His Majesty's Government are anxious to hand over their responsibilities to a Government which, resting on the sure foundation of the support of the people, is capable of maintaining peace and administering India with justice and efficiency. It is, therefore, essential that all parties should sink their differences in order that they may be ready to shoulder the great responsibilities which will come upon them next year.

After months of hard work by the Cabinet Mission a great measure of agreement was obtained as to the method by which a constitution should be worked out. This was embodied in their statements of May last. His Majesty's Government then agreed to recommend to Parliament a constitution worked out, in accordance with the proposals made therein, by a fully representative Constituent Assembly. But if it should appear that such a constitution will not have been worked out by a fully representative Assembly before the time mentioned in paragraph 7, His Majesty's Government will have to consider to whom the powers of the Central Government in British India should be handed over, on the due date, whether as a whole to some form of Central Government for British India or in some areas to the existing Provincial Governments, or in such other way as may seem most reasonable and in the best interests of the Indian people.

Although the final transfer of authority may not take place until June 1948, preparatory measures must be put in hand in advance. It is important that the efficiency of the civil administration should be maintained and that the defence of India should be fully provided for. But inevitably, as the process of transfer proceeds, it will become progressively more difficult to carry out to the letter all the provisions of the Government of India Act, 1935. Legislation will be introduced in due course to give effect to the final transfer of power.

In regard to the Indian states, as was explicitly stated by the Cabinet Mission, His Majesty's Government do not intend to hand over their powers and obligations under paramountcy to any Government of British India. It is not intended to bring paramountcy, as a system, to a conclusion earlier than the date of the final transfer of power, but it is contemplated that for the intervening period the relations of the Crown with individual states may be adjusted by agreement.

His Majesty's Government will negotiate agreements in regard to matters arising out of the transfer of power with the representatives of those to whom they propose to transfer power.

His Majesty's Government believe that British commercial and industrial interests in India can look forward to a fair field for their enterprise under the new conditions. The commercial connection between India and the United Kingdom has been long and friendly, and will continue to be to their mutual advantage.

His Majesty's Government cannot conclude this statement without expressing on behalf of the people of this country their goodwill and good wishes towards the people of India as they go forward to this final stage in their achievement of self-government. It will be the wish of everyone in these islands that, notwithstanding constitutional changes, the association of the British and Indian peoples should not be brought to an end; and, they will wish to continue to do all that is in their power to further the well-being of India.

Appendix 4

Preface
To the Second Edition by
Dr. Mohan Dharia

Shri Deva Chandra Jha was my Private Secretary when I was Minister for Public Works, Housing and Urban Development in the Central Government. I could have selected one of the officers from the IAS cadre for the post. However, as I was interested in a close interaction with the public, I avoided selecting an officer from the cadre and instead preferred D. C. Jha for the post, as his background suited my need.

D. C. Jha had joined one of Gandhiji's ashrams near Calcutta (now Kolkata) at a very young age. He was only 20 when he had an opportunity to get included in the party which accompanied Gandhiji to riot-torn district of Noakhali in the eastern part of the then united Bengal, now part of Bangladesh. Large-scale murder, looting, arson and conversion took place there after the Great Calcutta Killings of August 1946, resulting from observation of "Direct Action" day by Muslim League Government of Bengal.

Mahatma Gandhi had accepted the challenge to reestablish peace and harmony in this area where humanity was on fire and dared the danger of getting himself burnt in that fire, if necessary. During this crucial period, D. C. Jha was entrusted with the special responsibility of taking and delivering a confidential letter from Mahatma Gandhi personally to Dr. Rajendra Prasad, who subsequently became the first President of India, and bringing back and delivering personally his response and report to Gandhiji, who had by then begun to stay alone in one of the riotaffected villages with only a Bengali interpreter and his stenographer. One has only to imagine to understand the significance of a twenty-year-old boy, sitting all by himself across the

Mahatma, giving him the report on Bihar situation and answering the Mahatma's searching questions.

During 1974-75 agitations were witnessed all over the country on serious issues like unemployment, corruption and purposeful educational system. My request to Smt. Indira Gandhi, the then Prime Minister, that she should have a dialogue with Shri Jayaprakash Narayan on these issues to device a national programme, broadly acceptable to all parties, was not appreciated by her and the spineless Congress leadership, as I always believed that dialogue is the soul of democracy. I, therefore, resigned my ministership and continued my campaign for a dialogue.

I firmly opposed the emergency clamped with selfish intention to retain power. As a consequence, I had to travel from the Central Hall of Parliament at Delhi to the Central Jail at Nashik. During that critical period Shri Jha stood by me as a family member and our fabric of friendship has strengthened over the years. I am one of the privileged persons to have close friends like Deva Chandraji, from Kashmir to Kanyakumari, Kohima to Kutch and Chandigarh to Chennai.

I had closely observed D. C. Jha involved in reading, researching and writing in the library of the India International Centre in Delhi. When he told me that he was engaged in writing a book on Mahatma Gandhi and the partition of the country, I advised him that every statement made in the book should be based on records, undisputed facts, evidence and references. Shri Jha accepted my advice and produced his book of which the second edition is now being published. His effort has been appreciated all over the country and abroad as well. After reading his book I felt that it should be translated in Marathi and other languages.

Out of hatred and ignorance, without studying the facts, the background or events, the crazy youth, Nathuram Godse from Maharashtra, assassinated Mahatma Gandhi on January 30, 1948. Some fanatic families and friends have been trying to glorify this heinous crime. The controversial play, in Marathi, Me Nathuram Godse Boltoy, is nothing but a clear manifestation of the fascist communal tendency. During the period when the play was being popularised, I felt that people in Maharashtra should know the real facts and also the relentless efforts of Gandhiji who opposed the partition of India and was not responsible for the partition. My late friend Shri Madhukaka Kulkarni of Shri Vidyaprakashan came forward to gladly accept the responsibility of publishing the book in Marathi.

The book consisting of eight chapters and appendices, and the reference to books and documents, helps in understanding the bitter truth that leaders like Pandit Nehru and Sardar Patel were terrified by the communal riots and anxious to secure power were mainly responsible for the partition of India and not Mahatma Gandhi. Mahatma Gandhi totally opposed the partition and suggested to the British Government to hand over the power of independent India to any Indian party of their choice. He also announced that he was prepared to face any consequences.

Lord Mountbatten, the representative of the British emperor, who was trying to divide India got thoroughly frustrated and informed the Prime Minister of England that Mahatma Gandhi was the real obstacle in executing their plan of partition.

Shri Jha has successfully established that Mahatma Gandhi was not responsible for the partition of India. Without understanding this background, the act of assassin Nathuram Godse had no justification except the hatred shown in unity and integrity of India and on the great philosophy of peace and humanity.

Martyrdom of Gandhiji has made him immortal as champion of peace and love like Gautam Buddha, Lord Mahavir and Jesus Christ. His thoughts and preachings will always be remembered and serve as a guide to the future generations of the world. Attempts of transforming a murderer into a martyr are possible in India because of our liberal democracy. The nations that feel themselves powerful by acquiring military power with atom or nuclear bombs know perfectly well that they cannot survive with such power and the world has no other alternative but to follow the message of peace preached by these great saints and masters.

I would like to congratulate and thank Shri Deva Chandra Jha for writing this historical book and placing before the people the bitter but true history about partition of India.

Pune
August 23, 2004

Mohan Dharia

Endnotes

CHAPTER ONE
Second World War and Indian Independence

1. Linlithgow's telegram to Amery, January 21, 1942. *The Transfer of Power*, vol. I, pp. 47-49.
2. Ibid., p. 50.
3. Attlee's memorandum to the Cabinet, February 2, 1942. *The Transfer of Power*, vol. I, p. 111.
4. Ibid., p. 110.
5. Ibid., p. 111.
6. Clark Kerr's telegram to Eden, January 24, 1942. *The Transfer of Power*, vol. I, p. 76.
7. Clark Kerr's telegram to Foreign Office, January 28, 1942. Ibid., p. 80.
8. Churchill's telegram to Chiang Kai-shek, February 2, 1942. Ibid., p. 113.
9. Clark Kerr's telegram to Eden, February 5, 1942. Ibid., pp. 120-21.
10. Churchill's telegram to Linlithgow, February 6, 1942. Ibid., p. 121.
11. Linlithgow's telegram to Amery, February 11, 1942. Ibid., pp. 148-49.
12. Ibid., p. 149.
13. Linlithgow's letter to Amery, January 27, 1942. Ibid., p. 62.
14. Farewell message, February 21, 1942. *The Transfer of Power*, vol. I, p. 233.
15. Indian Agent General's telegram from Washington to British Foreign Office, March 8, 1942. Ibid., p. 375.
16. Mackenzie King's telegram to Churchill, March 6, 1942. Ibid., p. 350.
17. Ibid., p. 349.
18. Churchill's telegram to Mackenzie King, March 18, 1942. Ibid., pp. 440-41.

19. Churchill's telegram to Roosevelt, March 4, 1942. Ibid., pp. 309-l0.
20. Roosevelt's telegram to Churchill, March 11, 1942. Ibid., pp. 409-l0.
21. Churchill's telegram to Linlithgow, March 10, 1942. Ibid., p. 395.
22. Churchill's telegram to Cripps, April 10, 1942. Ibid., pp. 721-22.
23. Amery's letter to Mackenzie King, March 17, 1942. Ibid., pp. 435-36.
24. Note of interview. Ibid., pp. 498-99.
25. Cripps' telegram to War Cabinet, April 10, 1942. Ibid., pp. 715- 16.
26. Maulana Azad's letters to Cripps, April 10 and April 11, 1942. Ibid., pp. 726, 743.
27. Linlithgow's letter to Amery, April 14, 1942. Ibid., p. 773.
28. Linlithgow's letter to Amery, May 1, 1942. Ibid., vol. II, p. 8.
29. Roosevelt's telegram to Churchill, April 12, 1942. Ibid., vol. I, pp. 759-60.
30. Churchill's telegram to Roosevelt, April 12, 1942. Ibid., p. 764.
31. Amery's telegram to Linlithgow, April 20, 1942. Ibid., p. 805.
32. India Office to Viceroy's Office, April 20, 1942. Ibid., p. 806.
33. Louis Fischer, *The Life of Mahatma Gandhi*, chapter 22.
34. Ibid.
35. Resolution of the Congress Working Committee, April 28, 1942.

CHAPTER TWO
Quit India: The Unlaunched Battle

1. Government of India's telegram to Secretary of State for India, May I, 1942. *The Transfer of Power*, vol. II, p. 6.
2. Quoted by Louis Fischer, *The Life of Mahatma Gandhi*, chapter 22.
3. Linlithgow's telegram to Amery, May 27, 1942. *The Transfer of Power*, vol. II, p. 133.
4. Congress resolution, September 14, 1939.
5. Louis Fischer, *The Life of Mahatma Gandhi*, chapter 22.
6. Ibid.
7. Ibid.
8. Record of discussion in Congress Working Committee. *The Transfer of Power*, vol. II, p. 162.
9. Louis Fischer, *The Life of Mahatma Gandhi*, chapter 22.
10. Resolution of the All India Congress Committee, May 1, 1942.
11. Louis Fischer, *The Life of Mahatma Gandhi* chapter 22.
12. Press interview, May 16, 1942. *The Transfer of Power*, vol. II, p. 96.
13. Louis Fischer, *The Life of Mahatma Gandhi*, chapter 22.

14. Ibid.
15. Amery's letter to Linlithgow, May 28, 1942. *The Transfer of Power*, vol. II, p. 141.
16. Linlithgow's letter to Amery, June 8, 1942. *The Transfer of Power*, vol. II, p. 191.
17. Linlithgow's letter to Amery, June 15, 1942. Ibid., p. 213.
18. Louis Fischer, *The Life of Mahatma Gandhi*, chapter 23.
19. Ibid.
20. Quoted by Louis Fischer in *The Life of Mahatma Gandhi*, chapter 24.
21. Louis Fischer, *The Life of Mahatma Gandhi*, chapter 24.
22. Gandhi's letter to Linlithgow, July 2, 1942. *The Transfer of Power*, vol. II, p. 303.
23. Linlithgow's letter to Gandhi, July 5, 1942. Ibid., p. 308.
24. Government of India's telegram to Secretary of State of India, July 16, 1942. *The Transfer of Power*, vol. II, pp. 394-95.
25. Linlithgow's telegram to Amery, July 21, 1942. Ibid., p. 432-34.
26. Commander-in-Chief, Eastern Fleet's telegram to First Sea Lord, July 29, 1942. Ibid., p. 494.
27. Chiang Kai-shek's telegram to Roosevelt, July 30, 1942, Ibid., pp. 529-32.
28. Churchill's telegram to Roosevelt, July 31, 1942. Ibid., p. 537.
29. Government of India's telegram to Secretary of State for India, July 24, 1942. Ibid., pp. 447-50.
30. Government of India's telegram to Secretary of State for India August 3, 1942. Ibid., pp. 534-35.
31. Louis Fischer, *The Life of Mahatma Gandhi*, chapter 24.
32. Government of India's telegram to Secretary of State for India, July 24, 1942. *The Transfer of Power*, vol. II, pp. 447-50.
33. Louis Fischer, *The Life of Mahatma Gandhi*, chapter 24.
34. Roosevelt's remarks to Soong at Pacific Council meeting, August 12, 1942. *The Transfer of Power*, vol. II, p. 681.

CHAPTER THREE
Prelude to Partition

1. Pyarelal, *The Last Phase*, Vol. I, chapter II.
2. Eden's telegram to Campbell, August 7, 1942. *The Transfer of Power*, vol. II, pp. 608-10.

3. Eden's telegram to Seymour, August 7, 1942. Ibid., p. 612.
4. Chiang Kai-shek's telegram to Roosevelt, August 11, 1942. Ibid., p. 672.
5. Record of interview, August 11, 1942. Ibid., pp. 675-79.
6. Churchill's telegram to Roosevelt, August 13, 1942. Ibid., pp. 687-88.
7. Pyarelal, *The Last Phase*, vol. I, chapter II.
8. Ibid., quoted in notes for chapter II.
9. Minute of War Cabinet, August 7, 1942. *The Transfer of Power*, vol. II, pp. 604-7.
10. Amery's telegram to Churchill, August 8, 1942. Ibid., pp. 617-18.
11. Linlithgow's telegram to Amery, August 13, 1942. Ibid., p. 681.
12. Linlithgow's telegram to Amery, August 14, 1942. Ibid., p. 699.
13. Linlithgow's letter to Amery, August 24, 1942. Ibid., pp. 807-17.
14. Louis Fischer, *The Life of Mahatma Gandhi*, chapter 24.
15. Government of India's telegram to Secretary of State for India, August 3, 1942. *The Transfer to Power*, vol. II, pp. 534-37.
16. Linlithgow's telegram to Lumley, August 13, 1942. Ibid., p. 683.
17. *The Transfer of Power*, vol. II, p. 1003.
18. Ibid., pp. 985-86.
19. Linlithgow's telegram to Amery, October 12, 1942. *The Transfer of Power*, vol. III, p. 126; and Halifax's two telegrames to Eden, September 16 and 18, 1942, *The Transfer of Power*, vol. II, pp. 969-70 and 985-86.
20. *Harijan*, July 5, 1942.
21. Ibid., April 26, 1942 and June 21, 1942.
22. Ibid., May 3 and May 10, 1942.
23. *The Transfer of Power*, vol. II, p. 978.
24. Pyarelal, *The Last Phase*, vol. I, chapter II.
25. *The Transfer of Power*, vol. III, p. 268.
26. Ibid., vol. II, p. 536.
27. Ibid., p. 606.
28. Linlithgow's telegram to Amery, February 8, 1943. Ibid., vol. III, p. 420.
29. Gandhi's letter to Government of India, February 8, 1943. Ibid., p. 642.
30. Ibid., p. 671.
31. Linlithgow's telegram to Amery, February 17, 1943. Ibid., p. 682.
32. Telegram of Cordell Hull. Ibid., pp. 689-90.
33. Linlithgow's telegram to Churchill, Feburary 15, 1943., p. 669.
34. Linlithgow's telegram to Amery, February 15, 1943; Linlithgow's telegram to Governors, February 17 and 18, 1943. Ibid., pp. 668, 682, 684-85.

35. Churchill's telegram to Linlithgow, February 28, 1943. Ibid., p. 744.
36. Pyarelal, *The Last Phase*, vol. I, chapter III.
37. Louis Fischer, *The Life of Mahatma Gandhi*, chapter 22.
38. Pyarelal, *The Last Phase*, vol. I, chapter II.
39. Wavell's letter to Amery, May 1, 1944. *The Transfer of Power*, vol. IV, pp. 941-42.
40. Wavell's telegram to Amery, May 4, 1944. Ibid., pp. 948-49.
41. Pyarelal, *The Last Phase*, vol. I, chapter V.
42. Mukul Kesavan, *Looking Through Glass*, quoted in extracts published in the *Times of India*, January 29, 1995.
43. Pyarelal, *The Last Phase*, vol. I, chapter V.
44. Ibid., chapter VI.
45. Ibid., chapter VIII.
46. Ibid.
47. Ibid.
48. Ibid.
49. Ibid.

CHAPTER FOUR
Gandhi and Partition

1. Pyarelal, *Mahatma Gandhi—The Last Phase*, Vol. II, chapter II.
2. Letter dated February 10, 1947. Ibid., chapter I.
3. Letter dated March 25, 1947. Ibid., chapter II.
4. Letter dated March 24, 1947. Ibid., chapter II.
5. Record of interview. *The Transfer of Power*, vol. X, p. 69.
6. Alan Campbell-Johnson, *Mission with Mountbatten*, p. 44.
7. Record of interview. *The Transfer of Power*, vol. X, p. 84.
8. Record of Viceroy's staff meeting. Ibid., p. 145.
9. Letter dated April 5, 1947. Pyarelal, *The Last Phase*, vol. II, chapter N.
10. Record of interview. *The Transfer of Power*, vol. X, pp. 86, 121.
11. Record of interview. Ibid., p. 84.
12. Record of Viceroy's staff meeting. Ibid., pp. 126-27.
13. Record of Viceroy's staff meeting. Ibid., p. t27.
14. Record of Viceroy's staff meeting Ibid., p. 176.
15. Record of interview. Ibid., pp. 159, 163-64.
16. Record of interview. Ibid., p. 187.
17. Record of Viceroy's staff meeting. Ibid., p. 190.

18. Record of interview. Ibid., pp. 159 and 164.
19. Record of interview. Ibid., p. 164.
20. Record of Viceroy's staff meeting. Ibid., p. 177.
21. Record of Viceroy's staff meeting. Ibid., pp. 125-28.
22. V. P. Menon's note. Ibid., p. 24.
23. Alan Campbell-Johnson, *Mission with Mountbatten*, p. 57.
24. Record of interview. *The Transfer of Power*, vol. X, p. 70.
25. J. B. Kripalani, *Gandhi—His Life and Thought*, p. 280.
26. Letter dated April 13, 1947. Pyarelal, *The Last Phase*, vol. II, chapter IV.
27. Letter dated April 11, 1947. Ibid., chapter IV.
28. Mieville's note to the Viceroy, *The Transfer of Power*, vol. X, p. 199.

CHAPTER FIVE
Congress Breaches Gandhi's Trust

1. Broadcast to the nation on January 30, 1947. Pyarelal, *The Last Phase*, vol. II, chapter XXIV.
2. Nehru, Jawaharlal, *The Discovery of India*, 1973, p. 360.
3. Collins and Dominique Lapierre, *Freedom at Midnight*, chapter 5.
4. Letter to Sardar Patel. Rajmohan Gandhi, *India Wins Errors*, p. 37.
5. Pyarelal, *The Last Phase*, vol. II, chapter II.
6. Quoted by Amulya Ganguli in his article, *Times of India*, April 11, 1994.
7. Collins and Lapierre, *Freedom at Midnight*, chapter 5.
8. Letter dated June 16, 1945. *The Transfer of Power*, vol. V, p. 1133.
9. Letter dated June 12, 1946. Ibid., vol. VII, p. 886.
10. Telegram dated April 14, 1947. Ibid., vol. X, p. 231.
11. Record of interview. Ibid., vol. X, p. 70.
12. Collins and Lapierre, *Freedom at Midnight*, chapter 5.
13. Alan Campbell-Johnson, *Mission with Mountbatten*, p. 57.
14. Pyarelal, *The Last Phase*, vol. II, chapter IV.
15. J. B. Kripalani, *Gandhi—His Life and Thought*, p. 280.
16. Ibid., p. 248.
17. Collins and Lapierre, *Freedom at Midnight*, chapter 8.
18. Letter dated April 13, 1947. *The Transfer of Power*, vol. X, p. 800.
19. Letter dated May 17, 1947. Ibid., p. 862.
20. Letter dated May 31, 1947. Ibid., Vol. XI, p.11.
21. Dr. Ram Manohar Lohia, *Guilty Men of India's Partition*, p. 20.
22. Ibid., pp. 28-29.

CHAPTER SIX
Gandhi Considered Partition Preventable

1. Cabinet Mission's statement dated May 16, 1946.
2. Letter dated March 4, 1947 to Kanji Dwarkadas. Pyarelal, *The Last Phase*, vol. II, chapter IV.
3. Record of interview. *The Transfer of Power*, vol. VI, p. 830.
4. Letter dated March 25, 1947. Pyarelal, *The Last Phase*, vol. II, chapter II.
5. Alan Campbell-Johnson, *Mission with Mountbatten*, p. 87.
6. Pyarelal, *The Last Phase*, vol. II, chapter XII.
7. Dr. Ram Manohar Lohia, *Guilty Men of India's Partition*, pp. 52-53.
8. Ibid.
9. Alan Campbell-Johnson, *Mission with Mountbatten*, p. 57.
10. Letter dated May 8, 1947. *The Transfer of Power*, vol. X, p. 667.
11. Message sent through Rajkumari Amrit Kaur. *The Transfer of Power*, vol. X, p. 588.
12. Letter dated May 8, 1947. Ibid., p. 167.
13. Record of Viceroy's Staff Meeting, *The Transfer of Power*, vol. XI, pp. 3-4.
14. Record of interview. Ibid., p. 681.
15. G. N. S. Raghavan, *The Hindustan Times*, July 5, 1994.
16. *The Transfer of Power*, vol. XI, pp. 917-18.
17. Louis Fischer, *The Life of Mahatma Gandhi*, Louis Fischer, chapter 23.
18. Maulana Azad Abul Kalam, *India Wins Freedom*, epilogue.
19. Dr. Ram Manohar Lohia, *Guilty Men of India's Partition*, p. 50.
20. Zafar H. Jung in *Times of India*, March 5, 1996.

CHAPTER SEVEN
British Infamy Led to Partition

1. Record of interview The *Transfer of Power*, vol. X. p.588.
2. Ibid., vol. vm, p. 22.
3. Ibid., p. 709.
4. Record of interview. Ibid., p. 705.
5. Letter dated June 13, 1946. Ibid., p. 910.
6. Alan Campbell-Johnson, *Mission with Mountbatten*, p. 87.
7. Dr. Ram Manohar Lohia, *Guilty Men of India's Partition*, p. 52.
8. Record of interview. *The Transfer of Power*, vol. X, p. 159.

9. Alan Campbell-Johnson, *Mission with Mountbatten*, p. 44.
10. Record of interview. *The Transfer of Power*, vol. X, pp. 86, 121.
11. Record of Viceroy's Staff Meeting. Ibid., p. 86.
12. Alan Campbell-Johnson, *Mission with Mountbatten*, p. 57.
13. J. B. Kripalani, *Gandhi—His Life and Thought*, p. 276.
14. After-Prayer Speech, May 26, 1946. *The Transfer of Power*, vol. X, p. 1037.
15. Letter dated May 8, 1947. *The Transfer of Power*, vol. X, p. 667.
16. Record of interview. Ibid., vol. X, p. 611.
17. Note dated June 13, 1947. Ibid., vol. XI, p. 140.
18. Pyarelal, *The Last Phase*, vol. II, chapter XIII.
19. Report dated August 8, 1947. *The Transfer of Power*, vol. XII, p. 594.
20. Letter dated August 26, 1947. Pyarelal, *The Last Phase*, vol. II, chapter XVI.

CHAPTER EIGHT
Gandhi and the Congress

1. Nehru, Jawaharlal, *The Discovery of India*.
2. Pyarelal, *The Last Phase*, vol. II, chapter II.
3. Collins and Lapierre, *Freedom at Midnight*, chapter 5.
4. Broadcast to the nation, January 30, 1948.
5. Pyarelal, *The Last Phase*, vol. I, chapter VIII.
6. Ibid.
7. Ibid., vol. II, chapter II.
8. Collins and Lapierre, *Freedom at Midnight*, chapter 5.
9. Letter dated June 19, 1947. *The Transfer of Power*, vol. X, p. 508.
10. Telegram to Attlee dated July 2, 1947. Ibid., p. 826.
11. Viceroy's personal report dated May 1, 1947. *The Transfer of Power*, vol. X, p. 542.
12. Letter to Lord Listwell, dated July 25, 1947. Ibid., vol. XII, p. 331.
13. Ibid.
14. Letter dated June 11, 1947. Ibid., vol. XI, p. 279.
15. Pyarelal, *The Last Phase*, vol. II, chapter II.
16. Record of meeting, June 2, 1947. *The Transfer of Power*, vol. XI, p. 46.
17. Letter dated May 13, 1947. Ibid., vol. X, p. 800.
18. Letter dated May 17, 1947. Ibid., p. 862.
19. Letters dated June 2, 1947 and June 17, 1947. Ibid., vol. XI, pp. 68, 440-41.

20. Letter dated June 17, 1947. Ibid., p. 460.
21. Pyarelal, *The Last Phase*, vol. I, chapter VIII.
22. Ibid., vol. II, chapter XXI.
23. Ibid.
24. Letter dated July 28, 1947. Ibid., chapter XXII.
25. Letter dated July 28, 1947. Ibid.
26. Ibid.
27. Ibid.
28. Ibid.
29. Letter dated July 17, 1947. Ibid.
30. Rajiv Vohra in *Gandhi Marg*, January-March, 1994.
31. Pyarelal, *The Last Phase*, vol. II, chapter XXII.

*Everybody is today impatient for independence.
Therefore there is no alternative to partition.*

* * *

*And if I rebel against the Congress, it will mean
that I am rebelling against the whole country
because the Congress belongs to the whole country.*

– Mahatma Gandhi

Remembering Pyarelal
Mahatma Gandhi's Secretary and Biographer
Second Edition

Edited and compiled
By
D. C. Jha

Published by

KW Publishers Pvt. Ltd.
4676/21, First Floor, Ansari Road
Daryaganj, New Delhi -110002

www.ingramcontent.com/pod-product-compliance
Lightning Source LLC
Chambersburg PA
CBHW021357300426
44114CB00012B/1269